The Aborigines and Māori: The History of the Indigenous Peoples in Australia and New Zealand

By Charles River Editors

Mark Roy's picture of an Aboriginal artist

About Charles River Editors

Charles River Editors is a boutique digital publishing company, specializing in bringing history back to life with educational and engaging books on a wide range of topics. Keep up to date with our new and free offerings with this 5 second sign up on our weekly mailing list, and visit Our Kindle Author Page to see other recently published Kindle titles.

We make these books for you and always want to know our readers' opinions, so we encourage you to leave reviews and look forward to publishing new and exciting titles each week.

Introduction

A picture of Aboriginal dwellings in the 1920s

The Aborigines and Māori

"It is quite time that our children were taught a little more about their country, for shame's sake." – Henry Lawson, Australian poet

A land of almost 3 million square miles has lain since time immemorial on the southern flank of the planet, so isolated that it remained almost entirely outside of European knowledge until 1770. From there, however, the subjugation of Australia would take place rapidly. Within 20 years of the first British settlements being established, the British presence in Terra Australis was secure, and no other major power was likely to mount a challenge. In 1815, Napoleon would be defeated at Waterloo, and soon afterwards would be standing on the barren cliffs of Saint Helena, staring across the limitless Atlantic. The French, without a fleet, were out of the picture, the Germans were yet to establish a unified state, let alone an overseas empire of any significance, and the Dutch were no longer counted among the top tier of European powers.

Australia lay at an enormous distance from London, and its administration was barely supervised. Thus, its development was slow in the beginning, and its function remained narrowly defined, but as the 19th century progressed and peace took hold over Europe, things began to change. Immigration was steady, and the small spores of European habitation on the continent steadily grew. At the same time, the Royal Navy found itself with enormous resources of men and ships at a time when there was no war to fight. British sailors were thus employed for survey and exploration work, and the great expanses of Australia attracted particular interest. It was an exciting time, and an exciting age - the world was slowly coming under European sway, and

Britain was rapidly emerging as its leader.

At the time, the English were the greatest naval power in Europe, but they arrived on the scene rather later. The first to appear was William Dampier, captain of the HMS *Roebuck*, in 1699, after he had been granted a Royal Commission by King William III to explore the east coast of New Holland. By then, the general global balance of power was shifting, and with the English gaining a solid foothold in India, their supremacy in the Indian Ocean trade zone began. The Dutch, once predominant in the region, began slowly to lose ground, slipping out of contention as a major global trading power. So too were the Portuguese, also once dominant in the region. It was now just the French and the English who were facing one another down in a quest to dominate the world, but their imperial interests were focused mainly in India and the East Indies, as well as the Caribbean and the Americas. As a result, the potential of a vast, practically uninhabited great southern continent did not yet hold much interest.

By then the world was largely mapped, with just regions such as the Arctic Archipelago and the two poles remaining terra incognita. A few gaps needed to be filled in here and there, but all of the essential details were known. At the same time, a great deal of imperial energy was at play in Europe, particularly in Britain. With vast assets available even in peacetime, expeditions of science and explorations were launched in every direction. This was done not only to claim ownership of the field of global exploration, but also to undercut the imperial ambitions of others, in particular the French.

In 1769, Captain James Cook's historic expedition in the region would lead to an English claim on Australia, but before he reached Australia, he sailed near New Zealand and spent weeks mapping part of New Zealand's coast. Thus, he was also one of the first to observe and take note of the indigenous peoples of the two islands. His instructions from the Admiralty were to endeavor at all costs to cultivate friendly relations with tribes and peoples he might encounter, and to regard any native people as the natural and legal possessors of any land they were found to occupy. Cook, of course, was not engaged on an expedition of colonization, so when he encountered for the first time a war party of Māori, he certainly had no intention of challenging their overlordship of *Aotearoa*, although he certainly was interested in discovering more about them.

It was on October 6, 1769 that land was sighted from the masthead of the HMS *Endeavour*. The ostensible purpose of the expedition was to observe the transit of Venus across the Sun, but in sealed orders, to be opened only when these astrological observations were complete, he was instructed to search for evidence of the fabled *Terra Australis*. Approaching from the east, having rounded Cape Horn and calling in at Tahiti, the *Endeavour* arrived off the coast of New Zealand, and two days later it dropped anchor in what would later be known as Poverty Bay. No sign of life or habitation was seen until on the morning of the 9 October when smoke was observed to be rising inland, indicating that the territory was indeed inhabited. Cook and a group of sailors set off for shore in two boats and leaving four men behind to mind the boats, the remainder set off inland over a line of low hills. The sentries, however, were surprised by the arrival of a group of four Māori, who adopted an aggressive posture, and when one lifted a lance to hurl, he was immediately shot down.

Cook and his landing party hurried back, and after a few rounds were fired, the Māori retreated, and the party returned to the *Endeavour*. The next morning, however, another landing was made, and while some cautious communication was made possible by the fact that Cook had on his staff a Polynesian by the name of Tupaia, whose language was similar, the encounter was no less hostile. When, once again, an aggressive move was made by a Māori, a jittery sailor fired, and another Māori was killed. This was the preliminary to a more aggressive encounter yet, as the Māori attempted to board and kidnap a ship's boy, presumably with a view to eating him. A volley of shots was fired, however, and yet more Māori killed, after which Cook and his crew left the scene and continued their observations offshore.

The impression that all of this left on Cook and the scientific members of the expedition was mixed. By then there had already been several encounters with Polynesian people scattered about the South Pacific, and although occasionally warlike, there were none quite so aggressive as the Māori. In fairness, it must be added that the Māori understanding of Cook's appearance, and what it represented was by necessity partial, and in approaching it they simply fell back on default behavior, applicable to any stranger approaching their shores. The presence on board the *Endeavour* of Tupaia allowed for a certain amount of superficial exchange, and a little trade, but little else, and Cook was intrigued by this upright, warlike and handsome people.

Cook undertook two voyages to the region of the South Pacific, during which time the "Polynesian" triangle – Hawaii, Easter Island and New Zealand – was brought into the scope of European knowledge, so he and the scientists on board were able to claim at least some superficial appreciation of the Polynesian race. There was no doubt that the Māori, although heirs to a uniquely evolved society, represented a derivative of wider Polynesian society although how and when they made the vast crossing to New Zealand could hardly be guessed at.

Taking into account similarities of appearance, customs and languages spread across a vast region of scattered islands, it was obvious that the Polynesian race emerged from a single origin, and that origin Cook speculated was somewhere in the Malay Peninsula or the "East Indies." In this regard, he was not too far from the truth. The origins of the Polynesian race have been fiercely debated since then, and it was only relatively recently, through genetic and linguistic research, that it can now be stated with certainty that the Polynesian race originated on the Chinese mainland and the islands of Taiwan, the Philippines, Malaysia and Indonesia. Oceania was, indeed, the last major region of the Earth to be penetrated and settled by people, and Polynesia was the last region of Oceania to be inhabited. The vehicle of this expansion was the outrigger canoe, and aided by tides and wind patterns, a migration along the Malay Archipelago, and across the wide expanses of the South Pacific, began sometime between 3000 and 1000 BCE, reaching the western Polynesian Islands in about 900 BCE.

That said, the 19th century certainly wasn't exciting for the people who already lived in Australia. The history of the indigenous inhabitants of Australia, known in contemporary anthropology as the "Aboriginal and Torres Strait Islander people of Australia," is a complex and continually evolving field of study, and it has been colored by politics. For generations after the arrival of whites in Australia, the Aboriginal people were disregarded and marginalized, largely because they offered little in the way of a labor resource, and they occupied land required for European settlement.

At the same time, it is a misconception that indigenous Australians meekly accepted the invasion of their country by the British, for they did not. They certainly resisted, but as far as colonial wars during that era went, the frontier conflicts of Australia did not warrant a great deal of attention. Indigenous Australians were hardly a warlike people, and without central organization, or political cohesion beyond scattered family groups, they succumbed to the orchestrated advance of white settlement with passionate, but futile resistance. In many instances, aggressive clashes between the two groups simply gave the white colonists reasonable cause to inflict a style of genocide on the Aborigines that stood in the way of progress.

In any case, their fate had largely been sealed by the first European sneeze in the Terra Australis, which preceded the importation of the two signature mediums of social destruction. The first was a collection of alien diseases, chief among them smallpox, but also cholera, influenza, measles, tuberculosis, syphilis and the common cold. The second was alcohol. Smallpox alone killed more than 50% of the aboriginal population, and once the fabric of indigenous society had crumbled, alcohol provided emotional relief, but relegated huge numbers of Aborigines to the margins of a robust and emerging colonial society.

The Aborigines and Māori: The History of the Indigenous Peoples in Australia and New Zealand analyzes the origins of the groups, their histories, and the ramifications of their contacts with Europeans. Along with pictures of important people, places, and events, you will learn about the Aborigines and Māori like never before.

Prologue

"I have always found them of a brave, noble, open and benevolent disposition, but they are a people that will never put up with an insult if they have an opportunity to resent it." – Captain James Cook

On December 13, 1642, a Dutch survey expedition led by Abel Tasman and comprised of two ships, *Heemskerck* and *Zeehaen*, encountered in the South Pacific what Tasman later described as "a large land uplifted high." What Tasman was in fact looking at was the South Island of New Zealand, and the uplifted high land consisted of the Southern Alps. This land Tasman declared "*Staten Landt,*" or "State Land," and a few days later the small flotilla drifted into Cook Strait.[1] There the two ships anchored in a natural harbor now known as "*Mohua,*" or as it is known today, Golden Bay. There Tasman found a deeply indented shoreline and calm waters, fringed by wooded hills, and gifted with a mild and temperate climate. It certainly was a pleasing sight, and Tasman earmarked it as a country perfectly suited to future European settlement.

A contemporary portrait believed to depict Tasman and his family

---

[1] There are different versions of this naming. Another is that Tasman believed it to be connected to Argentina's Staten Island, or *Isla de los Estados.*

Then, quite unexpectedly, this utopian aspect was shattered when a flotilla of war canoes detached itself from shore and rushed out to meet them. A brief skirmish followed, and a few Dutch sailors were killed before a round of shots was fired that immediately dispersed the attackers. The sides separated and the natives returned to shore. They had never encountered ballistics before, so the experience undoubtedly scared them, but Tasman quickly hoisted sail and hurried back to open water. He later wrote of the encounter, "In the evening about one hour after sunset we saw many lights on land and four vessels near the shore, two of which betook themselves towards us. When our two boats returned to the ships reporting that they had found not less than thirteen fathoms of water, and with the sinking of the sun (which sank behind the high land) they had been still about half a mile from the shore. After our people had been on board about one glass, people in the two canoes began to call out to us in gruff, hollow voices. We could not in the least understand any of it; however, when they called out again several times we called back to them as a token answer. But they did not come nearer than a stone's shot. They also blew many times on an instrument, which produced a sound like the moors' trumpets. We had one of our sailors (who could play somewhat on the trumpet) play some tunes to them in answer."

Tasman named the place Murderer's Bay and continued on, arriving next in the Tongan Archipelago. To the Dutch captain, who had already touched the shores of *Terra Australis*, or "New Holland" as he left it, this first encounter with the natives of New Zealand was sobering. The Australian Aboriginals he had previously met were either friendly or semi-wild, fleeing to the bush like hares at the first sight of a white man. He had certainly never expected to be met on shore by a war party, and he immediately understood that anyone attempting to conquer and settle this land would certainly need to be prepared to fight for it.

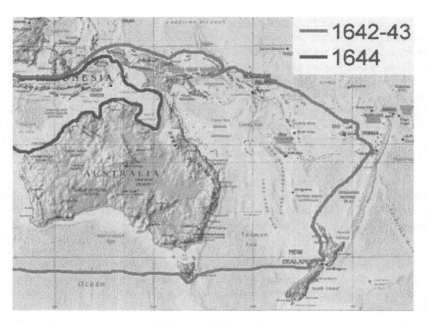

A map of Tasman's voyages in the region

A contemporary depiction of Murderer's Bay

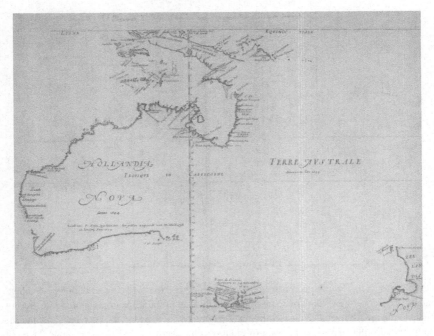

A 1645 map of the region

Archeologists have since explained this initial encounter as the unexpected arrival of an entirely unknown race into an area of settlement and agriculture, and the natural impulse that the indigenous people would feel to protect it. Nonetheless, this first European encounter with the Māori must certainly have presented a striking and intimidating picture. Warlike and tribal, the Māori were then, as they are now, flamboyant and decorative, fond of rituals and ceremonies, and accustomed to warfare as a cultural expression and means of inhabiting an accommodating land. Their distinctive tattoos, both erotic and totemic, were unique and striking expressions of a robust and violent, but also deeply accomplished society.

A 19ᵗʰ century depiction of Māoris

Abel Tasman has long been considered the first European to make contact with New Zealand and its people, but new scholarship has theorized that the first European encounter with New Zealand took place over a century earlier by the Portuguese. It was in the year 1498 that the first Portuguese flotilla arrived on the coast of India, seeding Portuguese settlements along the coasts of India and East Africa. It has since been discovered that a great many of the fundamental achievements in exploration attributed to British, and other European explorers, were in fact preceded by Portuguese travelers and explorers. In this instance, the basis of the theory is simply that Portuguese exploradores were simple and illiterate men, and many of their early feats of exploration were never recorded. It is also true that they explored the trade in slaves, and thus they courted anonymity. Quite often, Portuguese travelers and commercial explorers were simply Portuguese speaking natives or half-castes, and their work also tended to be disregarded.

The notion, therefore, of Portuguese ships making first landfall in Australia and New Zealand is not entirely outlandish. Upon rounding the southern tip of the Indian subcontinent, and crossing the Bay of Bengal, the Malay Archipelago forms a natural conduit in the direction of Australia. The Portuguese founded numerous settlements in these regions, most notably Timor, located just a few hundred miles across the Sea of Timor to the coast of Western Australia. There is also strong material evidence that the Portuguese were aware of the existence of *Terra Australis*, in particular in reference to the "Dieppe Maps," a series of sixteenth century French world maps that portray the "Java la Grande" as corresponding to the northwest coast of

Australia and scattered with Gallicized Portuguese place names. Artifacts thought to be of Portuguese origin have also been unearthed in adjacent coastal regions, and so the theory of prior Portuguese discovery of Australia, if not New Zealand, carries water. It is certainly not a great leap of imagination then to suppose that Portuguese ships, having come this far, might cross the Tasman Sea and set eyes on New Zealand.

Curiously, evidence of very early Spanish visits to New Zealand is a little bit stronger. In the northern Spanish city of La Coruna, a "pohutukawa" tree, native only to New Zealand, can be found. This specimen is estimated to be between 400 and 500 years old, and it is hard to imagine how a tree like that reached the Spanish coast unless a Spanish ship had collected it.

Either way, the first map to feature the name *Nova Zeelandia* was published by the Dutch in 1645, and no substantive European effort was made to exploit or visit this territory until at least a century later. After Abel Tasman, the next recorded European visit would be that of Captain James Cook.

The Land Before the White Man

"We are all visitors to this time, to this place. We are just passing through. Our purpose is to observe, to learn, to grow, to love…and then we return home." – Aboriginal proverb

The precise point at which mankind appeared on the Australian landmass remains a subject of debate, but current archaeology dates the earliest human presence at about 50,000 years ago. Other sources speculate a date of some 60,000 years ago, and others push back the date yet further to 100,000-125,000 years ago.

Aboriginal people have been present in Australia for between 50,000 and 120,000 years, a wildly divergent figure. Within that vast range of time, Australia, Tasmania and New Guinea formed a single continent known as Sahul, separated from the Asian mainland by a series of troughs that were never exposed by fluctuating sea levels. The human colonization of Sahul is thought to have taken place as a consequence of between eight and ten distinct waves of sea crossing. The uniqueness of the Australian fossil records has led to the theory that Australians and Papuans formed part of an earlier migration out of Africa that preceded that which founded the Eurasian population, but this, again, remains a matter of speculation. Recent genomic studies have tended to prove that the ancestors of modern Aboriginal Australians and Papuans admixed to a considerable degree with Neanderthal and Denisovan archaic hominins after leaving Africa.

By what route the first hominids arrived in Australia is another area of debate. Two possible options have been suggested, these being the northern route, in other words moving south from Papua and entering the Australian landmass via modern-day Cape York, or a more southerly course that would have passed through Timor into northwestern Australia. The former, however, is generally regarded as the most probable. The land bridge between Papua and Cape York flooded for the last time about 10,000 years ago, creating the Torres Strait, at which point a genetic separation was established between Papuans and Aboriginal Australians. However, as another illustration of just how conflicting opinion can be on this issue, the divergence of the two groups is nowadays generally set much earlier than 10,000 years, at 37,000 years ago, based on more recent genetic research. Papuans also tend to reveal higher traces of Denisovan genes than Australian Aboriginals which just adds to the confusion.

A possible explanation for this is landscape and climate. The enormous distances and hostile conditions of central Australia could certainly have created conditions for separation, and again, genetic research undertaken in recent years suggests a very wide difference between those in the north, who were more closely related to the Papuan race, and those in the south. These genetic variations are greater, for example, than the differences between Native Americans and Native Siberians who share similar genetic origins, but were separated by the Bering Strait some 25,000 years ago. Widely separated populations, therefore, are not only kept separate by ocean barriers but also by mountain and desert barriers which can be no less formidable.

Moreover, at the end of the most recent glacial period, approximately 11,700 years ago, the drawbridge to the outside world was lifted, and Australia was largely separated from the rest of the world. Recent studies suggest that the founding population of the isolated continent comprised an uncertain number of men, but no more than 3,000 women, which is understood to be the minimum number required to produce the genetic diversity currently observed.

Within these widely dispersed populations, localized social sub-divisions only began to occur in more recent times. At a point perhaps within a few thousand years of the European arrival, human populations remained tiny, and as a consequence, they were dispersed over a vast geographic area. As populations grew, however, for reasons perhaps of climate and rainfall, individuals and groups began to come in increasing contact with one another, and they merged and mingled with greater frequency. This offered to the earliest whites a general uniformity of appearance and habits that belied the diversity of Aboriginal origins.

It must, however, be reiterated that no two studies or theories on this subject completely agree, and any detailed study is made even more difficult by the fact most of the coastal regions inhabited by the earliest Aborigines now lie under water and are therefore beyond the reach of archaeologists. Carbon dates, stone tools and shell middens do not offer a sufficient historical record upon which to draw any reliable conclusion, so all is speculation.

In its social and cultural context, Aboriginal life varied with environment, but in general, lifestyles were nomadic and political groups very rarely exceeded the scope of the extended family. Chieftainship was loosely affiliated with elders, and those of exceptional ability while on the whole society was egalitarian, with an equal distribution of responsibility and stature between men and women. Women generally provided the stable sources of food while men hunted, and women were generally the guardians of ceremony and ritual, and, of course, reproduction. Men, on the other hand, were equally engaged in childrearing, while family and clan decision making was a shared responsibility, and law, such as it was, was codified in Dreaming stories.

Any discussion on population levels at the time of contact with Europeans is also likely to stir up fierce debate, but the current estimate of the pre-European population of the Australian mainland suggest something in the region of 750,000-1 million people. Scattered over such a vast continent, this implies a thin and extremely dispersed population. As such, it is not in the least surprising that, despite certain obvious commonalities, a great diversity of culture, lifestyle and language existed in Aboriginal society. Some 250 local languages were spoken at the date of European arrival, and numerous sub-dialects.

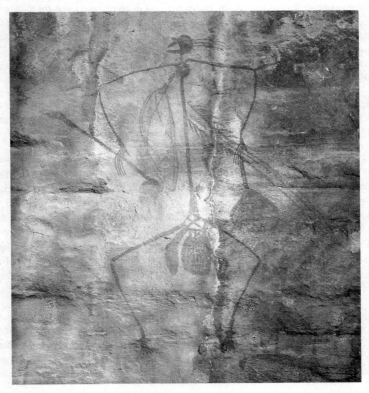

Thomas Scoch's picture of a cave painting that dates back about 30,000 years ago

Genetically, indigenous Australians are most closely related to the Melanesian and Papuan races, but Eurasian genetic indicators also suggest links with South Asian groups, perhaps influenced by more recent European admixture. According to a genetic study undertaken in 2011, there is evidence of the influence of archaic Denisovan admixtures. This study was followed up a year later by a second, the results of which hint at a significant genetic inflow from India, estimated to have its origins a little over 4,000 years ago. This coincides with the first evidence of tool manufacture and usage in the Australian archaeological record, and the processing of food, which to some archaeologists suggest a connected phenomenon. It is almost certain that the dingo arrived more or less at the same time.

According to an article published in the Proceedings of the National Institute of Sciences of the United States of America, "We find an ancient association between Australia, New Guinea, and the Mamanwa (a Negrito group from the Philippines), with divergence times for these groups estimated at 36,000 years ago, and supporting the view that these populations represent the descendants of an early 'southern route' migration out of Africa, whereas other populations in the region arrived later by a separate dispersal. We also detect a signal indicative of substantial gene flow between the Indian populations and Australia well before European contact, contrary to the prevailing view that there was no contact between Australia and the rest of the world."

Aboriginal contact with Asia came via the Malay Archipelago, and that influence was confined to a few points along the extreme north coast. Deeper inland, in the interior and along the east, west and south coasts, aboriginal societies existed in absolute isolation.

Aboriginal creation myths are as diverse as Aboriginal origin theories, but there are one or two common themes. The idea of "Dreaming," or "Dream Time," is a consistent theme of Aboriginal culture and spirituality. The "Dreaming" is a vague concept, as ephemeral as dreaming itself, but in general, it is explained as the time before human existence, in a dimension parallel to conscious life. It was a time or a space during which spiritual beings and hero-gods traveled across an empty land creating sacred sites and demarcating significant places. Language and other salient arts were distributed, and in some stories, the ancestors came up from the land, and in others, emerged from over the sea. Some ancestors were men and others were animals, while some were shapeshifters and could be either. Spiritualism was animist, engaged on multiple levels with the spirituality of nature and the cosmos.

Therefore, the Dreaming, or the "Ancestral Zone," exists, and it is tangible, accessible, and parallel to the conscious world at all time. According to indigenous Australian academic Helen Milroy, "We are part of the Dreaming. We have been in the Dreaming for a long time before we are born on this earth and we will return to this vast landscape at the end of our days. It provides for us during our time on earth, a place to heal, to restore purpose and hope, and to continue our destiny."

It is easy to appreciate the intense identification that Aboriginal Australian people have with the land. Its divine creation and preservation imbued a general landscape and specific aspects of it with almost immeasurable significance. As a result, the alienation of the land by European settlers during the 19th century was incomprehensible to Aboriginal Australians simply because the ownership and privatization of land had no basis of meaning. The land remains the property of the generations and cannot be individually claimed, with its sacred sites fenced off and separated.

Social and political boundaries were vague at best, defined and ratified by Dreaming creation stories, and an individual belonged to the land under very specific rules, not vice versa. Some writers have described the phenomenon of Aboriginal identity with the land as similar to a dog's, whose advanced olfactory abilities make real an entire spectrum of existence that people cannot fully perceive. Thus, it comes as no surprise that while the Aborigines didn't understand European concepts of land ownership, the early settlers couldn't comprehend the Aboriginal sensibility in regard to land, especially its invisible elements. An appreciation of natural spirituality, and the "inner eye," would have been meaningless to an average English convict or administrator.

Aboriginal social organization never rose to the level of organized political society, nor is there any evidence of any major societies along the lines of those that rose and fell in central and South America, Asia and Africa. Indeed, there seems to have been nothing even close to it. Social organization remained focused on family groups, for the most part nomadic within a limited range, or adapted to coastal life, and fishing. Those in the interior of the continent developed a simple hunter-gatherer lifestyle that remained almost unaltered until the arrival of whites.

Within this broad adaption to their various environments, aboriginal lifestyles and the material cultures of dispersed groups differed widely. The most concentrated aboriginal populations at the time of the European colonization were to be found in the southern and eastern sections of the continent, with the valley of the Murray River, at present in the southernmost mainland state of Victoria, and adjacent to Melbourne, hosting the most concentrated population. What was known as Van Diemen's Land before its conversion to Tasmania also hosted a small aboriginal population that did not survive very long into the era of European colonization.

Interestingly, in the extreme north, the avenue of original migration, there is evidence of a sustained trade between Makassan fishermen from Indonesia and coastal aboriginal clans that resided on the northern tip of Cape York. This would have inevitably catalyzed a certain amount of sophistication, and concepts of ownership, individual property and exchange. In the south and in the interior, nothing like that occurred. Without such concepts, and the inevitable social conflict that goes with them, it is easy to imagine that life, although short, was idyllic.

Then, one day, on April 19, 1770, a completely different kind of ship arrived in what would soon be known as Botany Bay. This was the HMS *Endeavour*, and on board, surveying the indented coastline through a telescope, was the 42-year-old Captain James Cook. Cook was about to make a signature discovery at precisely the right moment in history for the British, and his career was about to be immortalized, but it was also a discovery from which the indigenous population of the continent would never recover.

Cook

A replica of Cook's ship, *Endeavour*

A painting of the *Endeavour* leaving port on its expedition

New Zealand's First Arrivals

"Seek out distant horizons, and cherish those you attain." - Māori proverb

When and under what circumstances the first Polynesians arrived on the shores of New Zealand remains a source of acrimonious debate, and in the last century, the Māori's claim to first-nation status has been somewhat complicated by the possibility that an earlier, less developed population known as the Moriori populated the island of New Zealand long before the Māori and were driven to extinction by the more developed and aggressive Māori. Others claim that the Moriori were simply a branch of Māori.

A political overtone to much of this debate is inescapable. With no written language, the history of the Māori has been recorded and has tended to survive through oral tradition. Admirers and collectors of oral tradition frequently swear that oral sources are usually unimpeachable, and perhaps that is so, but the date and circumstances of the Māori's arrival nonetheless remain vague and incomplete.

A common misfortune of societies without a written language is that their history tends to be written by their enemies, and certainly the early leaders in Māori ethnography and chroniclers of Māori history were European. Among these was a renowned English ethnologist by the name of Percy Smith, who was only 10 years old when his family emigrated from England. Smith led the first efforts to gather and record Māori oral tradition, and through this process, he arrived at 750 CE as the most likely date of the first Polynesian contact with New Zealand. That said, he further postulated that the first substantial Polynesian settlement of the islands occurred about six centuries later, with the arrival of the "Great Fleet."

Smith

The Great Fleet was Percy Smith's pet theory, backed up by various versions of the story relayed to him through his research, but never categorically proven. Thus, it remains a theory to this day. In essence, the Great Fleet was believed to be a large and organized migration, embarking from somewhere in the region of the Cook and Society Islands, that arrived on the shores of New Zealand as an organized colonizing party. It may have been the first of many similar waves.

This version of the story asserts that around 750 BCE, a Polynesian explorer and adventurer by the name of Kupe arrived on the shores of an uninhabited land, leaving soon afterwards never to return. Three centuries later, Toi and Whātonga, also Polynesian explorers, arrived, and this time a primitive and nomadic race, the Moriori, had taken up residence. Presumably, the intelligence accumulated on both of these voyages was retained, for in 1350, a fleet of seven voyaging canoes (waka) arrived on North Island, originating from the region of Tahiti. These people, to be known by themselves as Māori, or the "ordinary ones," were a comparatively advanced, warlike and agricultural people, and before long they wiped out the Moriori and expanded to take over both islands.

Percy Smith established the basics of this idea, and thereafter it was generally accepted by both the Māori and Europeans. In fact, it remained the acknowledged version at least until the 1970s. Currently, the date of the first arrivals is set at 1280 CE, arriving from east Polynesia with a founding population numbering in the hundreds. Beyond that, not much can be added to the First Fleet theory, and as such, with one or two variations, it remains the most plausible.

Whenever the Māori arrived, they found a lush and forested land, with no particular extremes of climate or landscape, and with abundant wildlife. The latter included several now-extinct species of moa, a large and flightless bird weighing up to 500 pounds. Without natural land predators, the Moa were easy to hunt and became the first reliable food source. The bird is credited largely with providing a survival bridge between colonization and the establishment of viable agriculture. The moa was hunted to extinction, dying out sometime between 1300 and 1400.

The colder and more unpredictable climate of South Island created a somewhat greater dependence on hunting than agriculture, so the moa was hunted not only for food but also for its hide. From this, and the hide of the ubiquitous kiwi, came the unique feathered cloaks of the Māori. Seals were also commonly hunted, and foraging for shellfish and estuary fishing augmented a diet largely comprising yams and sweet potatoes.

A museum restoration of a moa

The sweet potato, the kūmara, was the main crop brought across with the early Polynesian settlers, and it proved viable under these new conditions. The Māori were generally skilled in producing agricultural implements, adzes and hoes, using stone and abundant hardwood, and it was not long before agricultural settlements were founded. The kūmara then became the basis of the Māori diet, in particular on North Island, where they grew well. It could be stored for long periods and eaten in combination with fish or other flesh. Other food crops were the taro, a starchy root crop, various yams, and the paper mulberry, which was used to make a type of bark cloth.

When the moa was eventually driven to extinction, Māori society was sufficiently established that alternatives were available. The kūmara remained the most important dietary staple, supplemented by fish and shellfish, and fishing became so central to the Māori domestic economy that strict conventions, or tapu, evolved in regards to who could fish where, when they could fish, and under what circumstances. These conventions still create tensions today.

While New Zealand's climate was for the most part nice, it was a great deal less benign than the islands from which they had come, and a more substantial style of domestic architecture was required. George French Angas, an English naturalist, explorer, and artist, was one of the earliest visual recorders of day-to-day Māori life, and he was eventually appointed Director of the Australian Museum in Sydney. Apart from copious observations and records, he produced a catalogue of watercolors of Aborigine, Māori, and African traditional life, and it is he who can be thanked for much of the visual records of Māori traditional life that exist today. He described an early Māori homestead, writing, "Sleeping or dwelling houses are partly sunk in the ground, and are always built with a gable roof and a verandah, where the occupants generally sit. The inner chamber serves as a sleeping-apartment, and towards evening is heated by means of a fire in the center; after the family enters for the night, the door and window are tightly closed, and in this almost suffocating atmosphere the inhabitants pass the night; when day comes, they creep out of the low door into the sharp morning air, dripping with perspiration."

Angas

In the early period of settlement, lifestyles were often nomadic, and homes as a consequence were at best semi-permanent. They were traditionally built in groups, with usually a simple wooden framework draped with reeds, bulrushes, or palm leaves, and occasionally with bark. Structures could be square, round, or oval, with earthen floors covered in mats, and with furnishings comprising bedding mats and little more. They were generally smaller than the typical Polynesian island style, with low doors and no windows, built often partly below ground level or heaped with earth around the sides. An interior fire usually provided for heat and cooking, with a simple opening in the roof to allow the smoke to escape. These dwellings were built in small, largely unprotected settlements known as "kainga," but by the 15th century, as settled communities began to develop, a more structured political organization was established.

One of the most striking features of traditional Māori society that whites noticed and recorded was their highly developed martial abilities. Warfare is embedded in the Māori creation myth, and a god of war, Tū or Tūmatauenga, is ubiquitous in Māori religious iconography.[2] Warfare tended to be internecine, with long traditions of conflict between groups and tribes (iwi), the origins of which were often lost over time. Indeed, by the time of the Europeans' arrival, Māori warfare had developed into a highly ritualized, almost religious observance. There are many living custodians of Māori history who will not accept the notion that Māori warfare was wanton and driven by an excess of violence, which is how the likes of Percy Smith and George French Angas were apt to describe it. Instead, it is described as simply a byproduct of a society displaying a preference for smaller, independent political and family units. Inevitably, under this social arrangement, squabbles and occasional conflagrations over land and natural resources would arise, and these, it is said, were typically resolved by diplomacy, with warfare only as a last resort.

That may well have been the case, but the imagery of warfare and the countenance of the god of war all tend to suggest a highly developed ideal of war and its associated rites of passage, and a highly theatrical tradition of martial display. The net result, regardless of what place war occupied in society, was the replacement of loosely configured and semi-nomadic kainga with fortified settlements known as pā. These ranged from simple defensive settlements to elaborate hill forts and permanent fortified villages. By then, Māori architecture had developed in sophistication, and permanent settlements and communities were a great deal more substantial. A communal sleeping house, or wharepuni, became the focus of the kainga, and therein several families could be accommodated each night. Typically, these were unadorned, although if the building happened to belong to a leader or community elder, his prestige, or "mana," might be illustrated with elaborately carved lintels (pare), pillars (poutokomanawa), or figurines (tekoteko). Often a porch or portico was included as an intermediate zone, which is a uniquely Māori adaption to the standard South Pacific communal dwelling.

---

[2] There are numerous Māori deities, some thirty-six formally listed, ranging from fire gods to sea gods, and gods governing various phases of life.

A depiction of a pā

Other buildings associated with a pā or fortified kainga was a common storehouse, pātaka, and a kāuta, or a simple outdoor kitchen.

Within these structures, a complex society resided. In classic Māori society, the largest political unit was the iwi, or tribe. Few if any examples of federations were ever recorded. Alliances were periodically formed between iwi of the same "canoe," but these were usually military alliances that were formed for the duration of a particular campaign, and rarely amounted to an authentic confederacy.[3] While the iwi was the largest political unit, it certainly was not the most important, for while individuals might give allegiance to the chief or leader of their iwi, their primary loyalty lay always with the hapū, a sub-tribe made up of extended family groups known as wahanau. The leader of a hapū was an Ariki, or chief, who derived his authority from his mana, itself inherited from his ancestors. The concept of "mana" is difficult to quantify outside of Māori idiom, and it perhaps shares superficial similarities to words such as "kismet" and "mojo" in terms of a combination of earthly rank, authority, and prestige, with more esoteric spiritual powers and inherited charisma. Mana as a concept lies very much at the heart of Māori society, and very frequently at the root of wars and conflicts. Mana is related to the concept of "utu," which is defined as reciprocation, or balance. In other words, every reaction must have an

---

[3] The Māori origin story claims the arrival of seven original canoes, or waka, from which the original identity of the tribes are drawn. To be of the same canoe implies part of the seven original iwe.

equal and appropriate reaction. If mana is greeted with kindness, utu demands kindness in return. If, however, mana is offended by violence, deceit or aggression, then utu demands similar reciprocation,which is simply revenge. That revenge, customarily, would wholly exceed the extent of the original injury, and thus utu had a tendency to proliferate and expand far beyond even the memory of the original insult or slight. It was of profound importance that an iwi's mana remain in balance, for mana was ultimately derived from the gods, and without it, an iwi was impotent in both war and peace, and would inevitably perish as a consequence.

If and when an important decision affecting the hapū required discussion, a public meeting was usually held on the marae, or village square, generally located in front of the wharerunanga or central meeting house. Here, various family heads, or kaumatua, were invited to speak, although the Ariki spoke first and last, and his decision on any matter was final.

Within society, there existed certain guilds, or tohunga, specializing in the skilled tasks associated with daily life. These, for example, could be building or woodcarving, or perhaps fishing, agriculture, hunting, or the manufacture of garments and tools. A large part of the function of a tohunga was to act as an archivist for the rituals and processes associated with a specific craft, and such rituals were central to almost every aspect of life. Each tohunga, therefore, was endowed with the function and powers of a medium or priest. Collectively, all of this was grail of tribal history, and a point of contact with Io Matua Kore, or the Supreme Being.

Absent from the built environment, however, was any kind of structure, gathering place, or large shrine to honor any religion. Indeed, Māori religion, in all of its many facets, has left very little material trace. The modest tuahu, or altars, still occasionally in use, hardly compete with the type of massive iconography associated with Easter Island or Tahiti, for example.

Another field of detailed anthropological study undertaken in the early years regarded the Māori concepts of ownership, and in the matter of proprietorship and property, it was generally believed that a kind of collectivism was practised without individual property rights at all. This has now come to be regarded as an oversimplification, and while such individual property rights were limited to possession, slaves, and occasional natural objects of spiritual importance, they were important and zealously protected. Land, however, was somewhat different. The land was Papa, the earth goddess from whom all Māori descended, so no concept of individual land ownership existed at all. The land was like the air and the water. The only avenue of land alienation was warfare and conquest, and land required occupation and tillage before it could be deemed that the correct "relationship" had been established. This, again, is an oversimplification, but the complexities of the Māori relationship with the land, notwithstanding certain common themes, tend to defy any single umbrella definition.

When the first contacts were made between European mariners and Māori and the whites observed their aggressive and warlike tendencies, they were often impressed by the Māori aptitude for trade. Intertribal and community trade was widespread, and based on the simple concept of homai o homai, or "a gift for a gift." In simple terms, an individual or delegation representing an iwi or a hapū, visiting another would bring an array of gifts, usually selected with a view to what their hosts would most appreciate. Coastal dwellers, for example, would offer fish, while inland dwellers might offer potted birds and rats. Hapū with particular artisans and skills might exchange carvings, tools, weapons or garments. None of this was conducted in the spirit of barter, but utu, requiring reciprocation, and hence an exchange, and often that reciprocation was larger and greater, requiring further reciprocation, and so on.

Thus, as Europeans appeared on the scene and began to introduce such fundamentals, as well as knives and axes, pots and mirrors, and glass beads and other decorative items, the Māori were quick to pick up the concept and willingly began to acquire and produce what was demanded in exchange. Before long, an item of magnificent utility was placed in the hands of the Māori, and soon after that, the sound of gunfire began to ring with ever-increasing frequency in the villages and valleys of both islands.

Initial Contacts with Europeans

In 1767, the Royal Society persuaded King George III to allocate funds for it to send an astronomer to the Pacific, and on January 1, 1768, the London Annual Register reported, "Mr. Banks, Dr. Solander, and Mr. Green the astronomer, set out for Deal, to embark on board the Endeavour, Captain Cook, for the South Seas, under the direction of the royal society, to observe the transit of Venus next summer, and to make discoveries." Mr. Banks was Joseph Banks, a botanist, and he brought along Dr. Daniel Solander, a Swedish naturalist. Charles Green was at that time the assistant to Nevil Maskelyne, the Astronomer Royal. The expedition, which would leave later in 1768, would be captained by Cook, a war veteran who had recently fought in the French & Indian War against the French in North America.

King George III

Banks

Solander

What the article did not mention was that the Admiralty was also hoping to find the famed Terra Australis Incognita, the legendary "unknown southern land." This came out later, when the *London Gazetteer* reported on August 18, 1768, "The gentlemen, who are to sail in a few days for George's Land, the new discovered island in the Pacific ocean, with an intention to observe the Transit of Venus, are likewise, we are credibly informed, to attempt some new discoveries in that vast unknown tract, above the latitude 40."

As this suggests, the British already knew that there was a mostly unexplored landmass in the region, and this is because Europeans had sighted the coast of Australia over 150 years earlier. The earliest entry by Europeans upon the Indian Ocean was by the Portuguese mariner Bartholomew Dias, who rounded the Cape of Storms (later the Cape of Good Hope) in 1488. He ventured no further than the confluence of the Atlantic and Indian Oceans, and it would not be for another decade that his compatriot Vasco da Gama pressed his discoveries further east to the coast of India. The Portuguese then established a presence on the east coast of Africa, and with the entire Orient to themselves, undertook numerous voyages of exploration, not all of which were directly recorded. There is, therefore, a school of thought advocating the notion that it was the Portuguese who were the first Europeans to lay eyes on the great southern land. Supporting this theory are ancient Portuguese maps of a coast that may well be Australia, and occasional relics of Portuguese origin that have been found in various places in Australia.

Perhaps the most compelling argument in favor of prior Portuguese discovery is logic. The Portuguese established colonies in India and various other points in Southeast Asia, with Portuguese Timor a mere 400 miles from the Australian coast. Bearing in mind the scope of Portuguese maritime exploration, there is no reason at all to assume that the Portuguese would not have followed the natural progression of the Malay Archipelago to arrive precisely on the north shore of Terra Australis. This would certainly be in character, and as early Portuguese mariners cruised the Malay Archipelago, it seems almost inevitable that they would have bumped into Australia. They could hardly have conceived of what it was, but it would nonetheless have given them prior claim.

Nonetheless, in the end, it was Dutch mariner Willem Janszoon, aboard the Dutch East India Company vessel Duyfken, who claimed those laurels. It is now an accepted fact that his expedition was the first to touch the shores of what would today be the northern tip of Queensland.

Janszoon was followed very soon afterwards by a Spanish expedition led by Portuguese navigator Pedro Fernandes de Queirós. This small fleet arrived from the east, having made numerous smaller discoveries en route around Cape Horn. Queirós in fact mistakenly took the New Hebrides to be the much-storied southern continent, so he named it Austrialia del Espiritu Santo, or the Southern Land of the Holy Spirit, in honor of the Spanish queen Margaret of Austria. The next to broach the horizon was a subordinate captain of Queirós named Luís Vaz de Torres, who sailed in from the east in July 1606. Sticking to the south shore of Papua, New Guinea, he passed through Torres Strait, which was subsequently named after him. He paused briefly on the northern tip of Cape York before continuing on through the Malay Archipelago.

For the remainder of the 17th century, frequent Dutch visits would be made to the coast of this vast and enigmatic land, and thanks to this it was nominally claimed by the Dutch, who called it New Holland. They were not disposed to settle and colonize, however; the Dutch were primarily a mercantile people, and their objectives were gold, spices, slaves, and occasional Christian missionary work. The coast of Australia appeared to have nothing of direct interest to these Dutch mariners, which ensured they moved on.

Thus, by the 1700s, the existence of the Terra Australis was generally known and understood, and incrementally, its shores were observed and mapped. With that said, the southern coast would not be mapped in detail until the 19th century, but Van Diemen's Land, an island off the south coast now called Tasmania, was identified in 1642 by Dutch mariner Abel Tasman. A few months later, this intrepid Dutchman would add New Zealand to the map of the known world.

The English were the greatest naval power in Europe, but they arrived on the scene rather later. The first to appear was William Dampier, captain of the HMS *Roebuck*, in 1699, after he had been granted a Royal Commission by King William III to explore the east coast of New Holland. By then, the general global balance of power was shifting, and with the English gaining a solid foothold in India, their supremacy in the Indian Ocean trade zone began. The Dutch, once predominant in the region, began slowly to lose ground, slipping out of contention as a major global trading power. So too were the Portuguese, also once dominant in the region. It was now just the French and the English who were facing one another down in a quest to dominate the world, but their imperial interests were focused mainly in India and the East Indies, as well as the Caribbean and the Americas. As a result, the potential of a vast, practically uninhabited great southern continent did not hold much interest.

Between the 1699 expedition of William Dampier and the 1770 expedition of the HMS *Endeavour*, little European traffic disturbed the epochal slumber of Australia. However, times were changing. As the *Endeavor* weighed anchor and slipped out of Botany Bay, Marie-Antoinette was betrothed to King Louis XVI of France, and the French Revolution was on the horizon. In the United Kingdom itself, the Catholic King James II of England had been overthrown by a coalition of Parliamentarians and the Protestant William of Orange, which triggered an economic and capital revival in England, the founding of the Bank of England, and a massive extension of the interests and influence of the mighty British East India Company.

By then the world was largely mapped, with just regions such as the Arctic Archipelago and the two poles remaining terra incognita. A few gaps needed to be filled in here and there, but all of the essential details were known. At the same time, a great deal of imperial energy was at play in Europe, particularly in Britain. Britain stood at the cusp of global dominance thanks almost entirely to the Royal Navy, which emerged in the 17th and 18th centuries as an institution significantly more than the sum of its parts. With vast assets available even in peacetime, expeditions of science and explorations were launched in every direction. This was done not only to claim ownership of the field of global exploration, but also to undercut the imperial ambitions of others, in particular the French.

One of these expeditions was the voyage of Captain John Byron, who rounded Cape Horn in 1765, but not before visiting and claiming, on behalf of the British Empire, the Falkland Islands as a strategic point of global navigation should the Dutch and the French have cause to deny British access to the Cape of Good Hope.[4] Then, in 1766, Captain Samuel Wallis was dispatched on a seminal expedition to circumnavigate the globe, and to find and annex New Holland to the

---

[4] In fact, a year earlier, the French landed on the archipelago and claimed it for France, and French diplomat and explorer, Louis Antoine de Bougainville, established the settlement at Port Louis on East Falkland.

British Crown. He did not succeed, but he met and passed on useful information to Cook, whose expedition followed soon afterwards.

Captain Byron

When Cook's expedition began in 1768, it included more than 80 men, consisting of 73 sailors and 12 members of the Royal Marines. Presumably, the expedition was supposed to be for entirely scientific – and hence peaceful – purposes. The *Endeavour* left Plymouth on August 26, 1768, and Cook landed at Matavai Bay, Tahiti, on April 13, 1769. The most important task at hand, other than day-to-day survival, was preparing to observe the transit of Venus that would occur on June 3.

Having completed the scientific assignments, the *Endeavour* next set sail in search of Terra Australis. After sailing for nearly two months, the crew earned the prize of being only the second group of Europeans to ever visit New Zealand. They arrived on October 6, 1769, and Cook described a harrowing experience when the men came ashore: "MONDAY, 9th October. ...I went ashore with a Party of men in the Pinnace and yawl accompanied by Mr. Banks and Dr. Solander. We landed abreast of the Ship and on the East side of the River just mentioned; but seeing some of the Natives on the other side of the River of whom I was desirous of speaking with, and finding that we could not ford the River, I order'd the yawl in to carry us over, and the pinnace to lay at the Entrance. In the mean time the Indians made off. However we went as far as their Hutts which lay about 2 or 300 Yards from the water side, leaving 4 boys to take care of the Yawl, which we had no sooner left than 4 Men came out of the woods on the other side the River, and would certainly have cut her off had not the People in the Pinnace discover'd them and called to her to drop down the Stream, which they did, being closely persued by the Indians. The coxswain of the Pinnace, who had the charge of the Boats, seeing this, fir'd 2 Musquets over their Heads; the first made them stop and Look round them, but the 2nd they took no notice of; upon which a third was fir'd and kill'd one of them upon the Spot just as he was going to dart his spear at the Boat. At this the other 3 stood motionless for a Minute or two, seemingly quite surprised; wondering, no doubt, what it was that had thus kill'd their Comrade; but as soon as they recovered themselves they made off, dragging the Dead body a little way and then left it. Upon our hearing the report of the Musquets we immediately repair'd to the Boats, and after viewing the Dead body we return'd on board."

Over the following weeks, Cook devoted himself to making a detailed map of the New Zealand coast. Sailing west, Cook hoped to reach Van Diemen's Land, known today as Tasmania, but instead, the winds forced him north, leading him and his men to the southeastern coast of Australia. As fate would have it, they were the first Europeans to land in this area. Cook recorded in his journal, "THURSDAY, 19th. At 5, set the Topsails close reef'd, and 6, saw land extending from North-East to West, distance 5 or 6 Leagues, having 80 fathoms, fine sandy bottom. ... The Southermost point of land we had in sight…I judged to lay in the Latitude of 38 degrees 0 minutes South and in the Longitude of 211 degrees 7 minutes West from the Meridian of Greenwich. I have named it Point Hicks, because Lieutenant Hicks was the first who discover'd this Land. To the Southward of this point we could see no land, and yet it was clear in that Quarter, and by our Longitude compared with that of Tasman's, the body of Van Diemen's land ought to have bore due South from us, and from the soon falling of the Sea after the wind abated I had reason to think it did; but as we did not see it, and finding the Coast to trend North-East and South-West, or rather more to the Westward, makes me Doubtfull whether they are one land or no. However, every one who compares this Journal with that of Tasman's will be as good a judge as I am; but it is necessary to observe that I do not take the Situation of Vandiemen's from the Printed Charts, but from the extract of Tasman's Journal, published by Dirk Rembrantse. ... What we have as yet seen of this land appears rather low, and not very hilly, the face of the Country green and Woody, but the Sea shore is all a white Sand."

Landing of Captain Cook at Botany Bay, 1770, by E. Phillips Fox (1902)

Cook next sailed the *Endeavor* north, exploring the coastline and making copious notes until he came upon a wide inlet, at which point the crew anchored and Cook and some of his men actually went ashore. Cook wrote, "Sunday, 6th. In the evening the Yawl return'd from fishing, having Caught 2 Sting rays weighing near 600 pounds. The great quantity of plants Mr. Banks and Dr. Solander found in this place occasioned my giving it the Name of Botany Bay. It is situated in the Latitude of 34 degrees 0 minutes South, Longitude 208 degrees 37 minutes West. It is capacious, safe, and Commodious; it may be known by the land on the Sea Coast, which is of a pretty even and moderate height, Rather higher than it is inland, with steep rocky Clifts next the Sea, and looks like a long Island lying close under the Shore. ... We Anchor'd near the South Shore about a Mile within the Entrance for the Conveniency of Sailing with a Southerly wind and the getting of Fresh Water.... The Country is woody, low, and flat as far in as we could see, and I believe that the Soil is in general sandy. In the Wood are a variety of very beautiful birds, such as Cocatoos, Lorryquets, Parrots, etc., and crows Exactly like those we have in England. Water fowl is no less plenty about the head of the Harbour, where there is large flats of sand and Mud, on which they seek their food; the most of these were unknown to us, one sort especially, which was black and white, and as large as a Goose, but most like a Pelican. On the sand and Mud banks are Oysters, Muscles, Cockles, etc., which I believe are the Chief support of the inhabitants, who go into Shoald Water with their little Canoes and peck them out of the sand and

Mud with their hands, and sometimes roast and Eat them in the Canoe, having often a fire for that purpose, as I suppose, for I know no other it can be for."

Cook also recorded his observations about the indigenous people: "The Natives do not appear to be numerous, neither do they seem to live in large bodies, but dispers'd in small parties along by the Water side. Those I saw were about as tall as Europeans, of a very dark brown Colour, but not black, nor had they woolly, frizled hair, but black and lank like ours. No sort of Cloathing or Ornaments were ever seen by any of us upon any one of them, or in or about any of their Hutts; from which I conclude that they never wear any. Some that we saw had their faces and bodies painted with a sort of White Paint or Pigment. Altho' I have said that shell fish is their Chief support, yet they catch other sorts of fish, some of which we found roasting on the fire the first time we landed; some of these they strike with Gigs, and others they catch with hook and line; we have seen them strike fish with gigs, and hooks and lines are found in their Hutts. ... However, we could know but very little of their Customs, as we never were able to form any Connections with them; they had not so much as touch'd the things we had left in their Hutts on purpose for them to take away. During our stay in this Harbour I caused the English Colours to be display'd ashore every day, and an inscription to be cut out upon one of the Trees near the Watering place, setting forth the Ship's Name, Date, etc."

A plaque commemorating Captain Cook's landing place

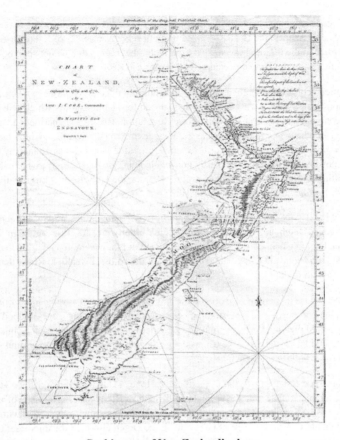

Cook's map of New Zealand's shore

As Cook sailed around the coast, he claimed every piece of land he saw for England. When he felt that he had found all that was worth finding, or at least all that he and his men could handle, he turned the *Endeavour* toward home. The ship arrived in England in July 1771, surprising many who thought that the ship must surely have been lost at sea given how long it had been away. Cook returned to a hero's welcome, with his journals instantly making him a celebrity among the intellectual elite in England.

Thus, it was Cook who would Anglicize the name to New Zealand, and on both of his subsequent voyages, Cook returned to New Zealand, but only to cruise the coast and touch lightly on the shore.

Cook's expedition may have been for the purposes of science on the surface, but when he claimed the new territory, the British realized it might serve as a center of future British maritime power and trade in the region. Indeed, as it turned out, that region that would soon be of significant interest to the British because of the American Revolution.

The American colonists, although patriotic and committed, could never have taken on the British Empire unassisted. A vast anti-British coalition formed in Europe, which provided the political, economic and material bulwark of the Revolution. Russia's Catherine the Great was the prime mover in what came to be known as the League of Armed Neutrality, which facilitated the free flow of money and materiel to North America, provided as aid and assistance by the non-belligerent powers. These, although hardly non-belligerent, included France, which was almost never unwilling to oppose the English, as well as Prussia, the Holy Roman Empire, the Netherlands, Portugal, Spain, and Ottoman Turkey.

After the 1783 Treaty of Paris, the British and the new United States somewhat reconciled, while the French, Dutch, and Spanish continued their bitterly anti-English campaign. In combination, they outstripped British maritime power, and they were in a position to challenge British trade with India and China, the cornerstone of the colossal wealth machine that was British East Indian trade.

At the time, the broad pattern of British trade saw British ships embarking south from England, sailing with the currents across the Atlantic, before striking east via the Cape of Good Hope to India. They would then load up on opium grown under duress by the Indians and ship it to China, where it was sold under duress to the Chinese. For the return journey, tea and various other exotic produce from India were acquired.

Vital to this trade equation was the Cape of Good Hope, a Dutch possession since 1652, and a pivotal strategic maritime position. As far as the British were concerned, the Cape of Good Hope was, at least for the time being, the weak link in the chain. The Dutch were allied with the French, and in addition to the Cape of Good Hope, the Dutch also held the important Ceylonese port of Trincomalee, from which they and their French allies were in a position to threaten British India and British trade interests throughout the region.

If push came to shove and the Cape of Good Hope became unavailable, the British trading fleet would be forced to utilize the east coast of South America, dealing with numerous Spanish and Spanish allied regimes inimical to the British, after which the Cape Horn or Magellan Straits would require negotiation before the long haul across the South Pacific to India. This would certainly not have been ideal.

Then there was the more subtle question of basic raw materials. The Royal Navy, the largest single maritime force in existence, had stripped the British Isles of timber reserves to the extent that a fleet of wooden ships could not be domestically sustained. British timber supplies that supported the local ship-building industries not only came mainly from Russia, but also other Baltic nations. However, in the aftermath of the American Revolution, Russia had become rather estranged and could no longer entirely be trusted. An average Royal Navy or merchant ship of the line utilized more than one mast, which was often several hundred feet tall, and these frequently required repair and replacement. So did the sails and the ships themselves. Denmark and Sweden, alternative sources of timber for the British, were also now of uncertain status, having signed on with the Russian sponsored pro-American League of Armed Neutrality.

It certainly was a hostile world for the British in the late 18th century, even as the British stood to benefit most from international trade. The Royal Navy and the British maritime fleet dominated the major maritime trade routes, but they did so from a position with almost no friends, and ultimately, if Britain could not rely on the cooperation of any other European powers, then the alternative was simply to make do alone. Cook happened to be of the opinion that the only major sources of timber and flax in the Pacific region were to be found in New Zealand and Norfolk Island, located some 1,000 miles northeast of Botany Bay. Nonetheless, it was his opinion that Botany Bay represented the most viable location for a permanent British colony.

Meanwhile, the anti-British alliance continued to ferment in the aftermath of the French Revolution. The French were deeply embittered by their ejection from North America, and for that matter, so were the British, but there was little to be gained by either side crying over spilled milk. However, the French remained deeply interested in India, which was still not comprehensively dominated by the British, and thus still vulnerable to a robust French effort at a takeover. In fact, the French were negotiating a treaty with Ottoman Egypt that would allow French use of Egyptian soil in general communication with her surviving outposts in India. Those outposts were fortified with apparently decommissioned gunships, and a military alliance was formalized with the Dutch for the use of port facilities at the Cape of Good Hope and other Dutch bases in the Pacific.

As a result, in the wake of Cook's voyages, a robust body of commercial explorers, consisting of European whaling fleets, began to probe the New Zealand shoreline for whales and fur seals. It was they who founded the first settlements, and they would be the first to make substantive contact with the Māoris.

Deadly Diseases

In 1785, the French mounted a "scientific" expedition to the South Pacific with the ostensible purpose of mapping and exploration. On board were some 60 French convicts, intent, according to British espionage sources, on establishing a naval base on the shores of New Holland.

When news of this reached the imperial establishment in Britain, it was gripped by the sudden urgency to establish a British colony before the French could get there and do the same. Leading the effort to take practical possession of New Holland was eminent British gentleman scientist and naturalist Joseph Banks, president of the Royal Geographic Society and a major figure in British exploration. Banks had accompanied Cook on his preliminary voyage to New Holland, and he was generally regarded in British circles as the leading = authority on Australia. Having earlier declared the territory unfit for British colonization, he now championed colonization with a furious passion. Supported by the Society and by the extremely influential board of the British East India Company, the British establishment responded quickly. Thus, on May 13, 1787, the "First Fleet" set sail.

The fleet of 11 ships was commanded by Captain Arthur Phillip, and a race with the French was on. It was not known precisely where the French fleet was, but it was understood, or perhaps hoped, that the hastily assembled British expedition had the jump. To be safe, three of the faster ships in the fleet quickly broke away, arriving in Botany Bay on January 18, 1788.

Phillip, a man of enormous competence and extremely decided opinions, felt, after a few days, that Botany Bay did not meet the needs of a settlement, so he moved the entire fleet a few miles north up the coast to Port Jackson. The expedition dropped anchor in a sheltered harbor, and the site was named Sydney Cove, now more or less the site of the Royal Botanical Gardens. The settlement that grew up around Port Jackson took on the name Sydney, in honor of the British Home Secretary Lord Sydney.

Phillip

Greg O'Beirne's picture of a statue of Phillip on the site

Meanwhile, the French fleet arrived in Botany Bay narrowly behind the British, and as they did, Phillip dispatched a small force to Norfolk Island in order to claim that before the French could gather their senses. The French lingered for a while, but the deed was done, and New Holland, demarcated by common understanding as the eastern coast of Terra Australis, was effectively British.

At least initially, this did not change much. The British had made preliminary landfall on the Australian coast and established a nascent colony, but that hardly opened the door to immediate dominance of the South Pacific. Nonetheless, it was a major moment in the imperial machinations of the age, as history would later prove. Technically, the British were now in a position to potentially project power across the South Pacific to Spanish America, but perhaps most importantly, the British could now challenge the Spanish claim to the northwest coast of the American continent. It also positioned the British to challenge French and Dutch holdings in the Far East, and to better protect British interests in India, which by then was emerging as the virtual treasury of the British Empire.

The British cover story for all of this was the establishment of an overseas penal colony, which fooled no one. This story, apart from the fact that it would in due course become a self-fulfilling prophecy, was aimed as much at opposition within the United Kingdom as to the French or the Dutch. There was a great deal of domestic opposition to the establishment of a British colony in such a remote location, and one so disconnected from Europe at that. Captain Phillip was installed as the first Governor of the Colony, the colony of New South Wales, which was formally established on January 26, 1788. Soon afterwards, Phillip wrote to his sponsor, Lord Shelburne, the ex-prime minister, that "it will be four years at least, before this Colony will be able to support itself. Still, My Lord, I think that perseverance will answer every purpose proposed by Government, and that this Country will hereafter be a most valuable acquisition to Great Britain from its situation." In both cases, Governor Phillip would prove right.

From the point of view of the early incoming colonists, both Aboriginal numbers and their signature on the land were so insubstantial that they were hardly recognized as anything more than a curiosity. They were regarded as too wild to tame and to itinerate for use as labor, besides which, the convict settlements had labor aplenty, and so where they occupied land, they were simply a nuisance. Then, as they began to actively resist European occupation and takeover of land, they became classified informally as vermin.

In the early days, however, extermination by force was hardly necessary, because smallpox was lurking in the holds of the British ships, and it was brought ashore by sick convicts. In April 1789, 15 months after the arrival of the First Fleet and the first colonists, the first smallpox epidemic began. Neither the convicts nor the colonists were affected in any appreciable numbers because they had a natural resistance to the infection, but this also had the perverse effect of ensuring that the extent of the disease among Aboriginals was not detected until whites began discovering the dead in and around the area of Sydney Cove, as well as numerous caves and inlets along the shoreline. The dead were typically found with the remains of a small fire on either side of them, and with food and water lying within reach.

Without resistance to the disease, smallpox almost destroyed the local Aboriginal population, killing upwards of 70% of them. In general, the impact on the small European population was slight, so it did not loom particularly large as an epidemic, and it attracted very little in the way of resources. What was taking place in Aboriginal society, on the other hand, was not only utterly catastrophic, but also largely hidden. The epidemic appeared to last only for a few weeks in and around the European settlements, but out of sight, it spread rapidly in both directions along the coast, and along trails and river corridors deep into the interior where no white man had yet ventured.

One who observed and wrote a great deal about it was the Judge-Advocate and Secretary of the Colony, David Collins. In 1798, he recorded this observation: "Early in the month, and throughout its continuance, the people whose business called them down the harbor daily reported, that they found, either in excavations of the rock, or lying upon the beaches and points of the different coves which they had been in, the bodies of many of the wretched natives of this country."

Most reports were similarly anecdotal, and they comprised observations of dead and dying natives as colonists went about their daily business. In June 1789, for example, Governor John Phillip led an exploration of Broken Bay, a large inlet formed by the mouth of the Hawkesbury River, about 10-15 miles to the north of the Port Jackson settlement. David Collins accompanied the expedition and wrote that the footpaths they followed were "in many places covered with skeletons, and the same spectacles were met with in the hollows of the rocks of that harbour." Another member of that expedition recalled more graphically his impressions as the expedition encountered a fishing party: "[T]hey all made their escape, except this miserable girl, who had just recovered from the small-pox, and was very weak, and unable, from a swelling in one of her knees, to get off to any distance ... she appeared to be about 17 or 18 years of age, and had covered her debilitated and naked body with the wet grass, having no other means of hiding herself."

The impact of the epidemic was most profoundly felt by the Eora people, a dispersed language group living close to the Port Jackson and Sydney settlement. No statistics, of course, were ever compiled, but Governor Phillip remarked in a journal entry, "It is not possible to determine the number of natives who were carried off by this fatal disorder. It must be great; and judging from the information of the native now living with us... one half of those who inhabit this part of the country died..."

A second major smallpox outbreak occurred about 40 years later, between about 1828 and 1832, by which time the colony of New South Wales and its satellites were in a better position to observe and take note. Consequently, this epidemic was more carefully studied and documented.

By then settlers and colonists had begun to explore the Great Dividing Range, leaving the precincts of Sydney and seeding settlements throughout the Bathurst Plains region. Along the river systems, heavily infected Aboriginal communities were recorded, with some carrying the disease and others with recent scarring. Oral accounts described the epidemic as extending much deeper into the interior, along the western flowing river corridors, penetrating ultimately as far inland as South Australia.

Yet a third epidemic was recorded in 1866-1867, mainly among the Nawu, Wirangu and Banggaria people inhabiting the western coast and inland regions of South Australia. This was probably the southern extent of an earlier epidemic originating on the north and west coasts, penetrating unsettled regions of the interior and therefore beyond the scope of official investigation.

Smallpox, of course, was not the only disease introduced to the natives by Europeans. The First Fleet also imported tuberculosis, which was even more prevalent among convicts, and although this disease took longer to establish itself, once it did, it far outstripped the scattered smallpox outbreaks in terms of steady attrition and numbers killed.

Sexually transmitted diseases were also spread into aboriginal societies, located as they were in places where there were more white men than women. Simple influenza was another. Again, general mortality rates were always a matter of guesswork, but many observers of the time, even in an age when sympathy for indigenous races was not conspicuous, expressed a sense of regret over the sheer number of people who died due to initial contact with European colonizers. There has long been a persistent conspiracy theory that smallpox was carried to Australia by way of vaccination material and deliberately released in order to eradicate the native population, but while this is a popular theory, there remains no evidence to support it.

The Frontier Wars

Notwithstanding the narrow parameters governing the settlement of the colony, adventurous spirits always looked beyond the first range of mountains, wondering what lay beyond. At that point almost nothing was known; the settled regions of the Port Jackson hinterland comprised an area comparable to Sicily in relation to continental Europe, and aside from the fact Mathew Flinders had confirmed that it was a continent and not an archipelago, even the outline of the coast was sparsely mapped and imperfectly understood.

The first probe into the great unknown was the Blaxland-Lawson expedition, which sought to forge a passage through the Blue Mountains, and that endeavor concluded in the discovery of the Bathurst Plain. The process then continued with the journeys of George Bass and Mathew Flinders.

Bass

Flinders

    The discovery of a practical route through the Blue Mountains set in motion an entire shift of attitude both inside and outside of the growing colony of New South Wales. From a thorough disinterest in immigration to the colony, other than for its essential administrative needs, the British government began suddenly promoting immigration, signaling in many ways the beginning of the end of penal transportation and the establishment of a more traditional British colony. All of this would take time since the administration of the colony was bedeviled by time and distance, but before long, it was the immigrant ship that slowly began to replace the convict ship as the most common sight in Port Jackson's harbor. The British press, now better informed, began reporting on the opportunities available in the new Australian colony, where land grants were easily obtainable and where a man of modest capital could lay claim to an acreage exceeding the wealthiest squires of England.

In the 1820s, Australia remained almost wholly unexplored, but more strategic points were identified and occupied. The settlement of Westernport took place between 1824 and 1827. Westernport, consisting of about 50 convicts, did not last for long, but Albany, similarly settled, did survive and eventually became permanent. The Melville Island settlement also did not endure for long but was moved soon afterwards to the mainland at Raffles Bay, the site of present-day Fort Wellington, where it became the basis of the city of Darwin.

In 1829, a momentous article of legislation was passed in the British House of Commons that declared the jurisdiction of the British governor general to be the entire Australian continent. In practical terms, this meant that Britain laid formal claim to Australia in total as an imperial possession. No one else was in a position to argue, and no one did.

The seeding of settlements, therefore, continued at a more measured pace, and in that year, Captain Charles Fremantle, commanding the HMS *Challenger*, entered the Swan River and dropped anchor in one of the most superb natural harbors in the world. This, the site of the future Perth, was claimed by Fremantle as part of the wider British claim to "all that part of New Holland which is not included within the territory of New South Wales." This, in essence, meant that the western half of the continent would theoretically be a colony separate of New South Wales. New South Wales, for the time being, comprised the entire eastern half of the continent, almost all of which remained completely unexplored.

Fremantle

George Pit Morison's painting of the founding of Perth

This would not be the end to the matter, but in the meantime, as men were dropped in lands entirely unknown and given the basic means to survive, they naturally began to probe more deeply inland to see what lay beyond the dunes and cliffs. As a result, most of the early explorers were merely settlers and homesteaders engaged in breaking the ground and establishing a widely dispersed system of smallholdings, farms and homesteads. There were certainly those, mainly later in the century, who undertook epic journeys of exploration, for their own sake and for the sake of science, but most of the map of early Australia was drawn by settlers themselves, adding to the body of knowledge in increments.

There has tended to be a persistent myth that the Aboriginal people of Australia passively watched as Europeans entered and took over their land. This might have been true on occasions, but almost from the commencement of white settlement, hostilities and difficulties characterized the early clash of cultures.

As the various settlements spread, the local Darug people, whose traditional land it was, began mounting periodic raids against settled homesteads. Members of the colonial militia were sent into the area, and civilian homesteaders were granted authority by the governor to shoot Aboriginal people displaying any hostile attitude.

In 1795, an organized resistance was mounted by a notable member of the Darug by the name of Pemulwuy who was able to negotiate a loose alliance between his group and the Eora and

Tharawai tribes. Here, indeed, is where the main Aboriginal weakness lay. The enemy, who were the colonists, were organized and united, while the Aborigines, in general, fought their own fight and rarely if ever allied to form a united front. Pemulwuy, however, was active for about six years at the head of an itinerate gang until a bounty was placed on his head, and in June 1802, he was shot and killed. The Hawkesbury and Nepean Wars, as this branch of the conflict came to be known, was ended when Governor Lachlan Macquarie sent in troops from the British Army's 46th Regiment who attacked an Aboriginal encampment and killed 14 people.

When the first settlement in Van Diemen's Land was established in 1803, relations between settlers and the local Aboriginal people were cordial. In general, the indigenous population was not warlike, but as European agricultural settlement rapidly spread, conflict over land was the inevitable result. By the 1830s, Aboriginal resistance on Van Diemen's Land had evolved into a coordinated and sustained operation that has been described as the most successful of the Frontier War period. In the border districts, farms survived only as minor fortresses, and practical farming was, for the most part, impossible. Numerous killings of settlers took place until eventually something had to be done about the "Black War."

Once a viable route had been established across the Blue Mountains and settlers began moving across and squatting on land on the fertile plains, they were immediately attacked by groups of the Wiradjuri people, who killed stockmen and livestock. This, in turn, attracted retaliatory raids that soon began to offend even British Governor Thomas Brisbane. Brisbane declared martial law in 1824, in order, as he put it, to halt "the Slaughter of Black Women and Children, and unoffending white men." Nonetheless, as the settlement gathered pace on the Bathurst Plains, and from about the 1830s onwards, the leading edge of this advance witnessed an ongoing struggle, with occasional massacres such as the Waterloo Creek Massacre and the Myall Creek Massacre. The violence collectively accounted for hundreds of lives, and small actions by the Aborigines were almost always met with disproportionate force. If there was an opportunity to wipe out a native population, that opportunity was rarely missed.

In 1836, a British Parliamentary select committee was assembled to investigate the conditions of aboriginal peoples in the colonies. The preamble to the report of the committee speaks somewhat to its mandate: "[To] consider what measures ought to be adopted with regards to the native inhabitants of the countries where British settlements are made, and to the neighboring tribes, in order to secure to them the due observance of justice, and the protection of their rights; to promote the spread of civilization among them, and to lead them to the peaceful and voluntary reception of the Christian religion."

This spoke to all the major settled colonies of the empire, comprising India, British North America (Canada), New Zealand, South Africa, and Australia. In every case an indigenous population lay in the path of European interests, and again, in almost every case, the results were detrimental to native societies. Some suffered more acutely than others. Indians and Africans did not succumb quite so easily to pernicious disease as the natives of North America and Australia did, and as such, once released from slavery, their numbers and general prosperity improved. However, they were still subject to rapacious European economic piracy, mostly in the seizure of their land, but also, in such colonies as Natal, in the unequal social restrictions that locked them out of normal economic development.

The formation of this select committee marked an important moment in British history, a moment in which the British Empire began to establish its essential charter. In view of British global dominance, that charter necessarily included the first official acknowledgement of a responsibility inherited by the British people to balance their global ambitions with the humane usage of the aboriginal peoples falling under British sovereignty.

In 1837, the Aborigine Protection Society was formed in England by a small group of British liberals with an interest in ensuring the protection of the sovereign legal and religious rights of native peoples falling under the Pax Britannia. This was a mere four years after the abolition of slavery in the British Empire, and this Society is often regarded as one of the earliest human rights organizations. Many of those active in the Society were also active in the abolition movement of a generation earlier, and this marked something of a sea change in European attitudes when it came to race and the responsibility of the empire.

In many respects, this was the essential enigma of the British Empire. In the post-slavery era, an enormous weight of conscience seemed to settle on the shoulders of the metropolitan population. In a generally liberal age, the British intelligentsia responded by seeking to ameliorate some of the worst impacts of cultural exploitation, especially once the grotesquely deleterious effects of European intrusion into new lands was understood. However, that sentiment, while powerfully expressed and felt in England, did not easily translate along the frontiers, where the practical work of founding an empire was taking place. The noble savage seemed often less noble in close proximity, and the ostensibly primitive lifestyles of those like the Australian Aborigines allowed them to be construed as something less than human, and therefore outside the social charter.

In due course, the colonial authorities in Australia would apply numerous policies of social engineering that affected the indigenous people of the federation. In the early years, however, no such finesse existed, and where the two cultures met, and where the Aborigines resisted, they were dealt with both arbitrarily and violently. For example, in Van Diemen's Land, under the governorship of Sir George Arthur, the extermination of Aborigines was pursued with vigor, even though the population was always small. Any elements that survived the onslaught of disease were mopped up later under an informal system of bounty.

Again, at odds with the popular view of Australia's Aboriginal people as a passive, spiritual and yielding race is the fact that warfare did indeed exist in their society. Although hardly on the scale of the Maori warfare in New Zealand, or the martial traditions of many South Sea Island societies, Aboriginal warfare took the form of violent skirmishes in pursuit of vendettas, women, natural resources, or local predominance. Aboriginal weapons technology was adequate for the needs of a hunter/gatherer society, but hardly the offensive equipment typically to be found in the hands of the Maoris.

It is also true that indigenous Australians, to a greater or lesser extent, lacked the scope of social organization necessary to mount anything resembling a conventional war. The experience of outward moving Australian pioneers and settlers could hardly compare, for example, to those of the South African Boer who were matched against the Zulu and the amaNdebele, two of the most effective and organized military societies in the non-European world. The Zulu, however, held a clear sense of land title (albeit communal), and they understood the concept and ramifications of white occupation. Concepts of Aboriginal land and land ownership, on the other hand, were vague and steeped in tradition. Although immensely valuable to them as a whole, conquering, occupying and defending territory simply did not exist as a concept. Likewise, the gathering of a confederation to fight a common enemy on a substantial level was also simply absent from the common mindset. The Aborigines of Australia, therefore, could hardly have been less equipped to deal with the arrival of outsiders.

Initially, however, the melee and ambush tactics of the Aborigines worked well. They easily matched the colonists' ability to defend themselves with the simple, muzzle loading black powder guns of the age. Things changed radically, however, at the moment that breech-loading and repeating rifles appeared on the scene. Mounted infantry and ad hoc settler militias began to deal ruthlessly and efficiently with the paper-thin defenses of vulnerable Aboriginal communities. Thus, the balance of power began to shift very quickly, and very much against the Aborigines.

What was known as the "Australian Frontier Wars" was little more than an ongoing attrition between the two sides that began almost immediately and continued well into the 20th century, with the last recorded fights being logged as late as the 1930s. Periodically the "war" flared into identifiable battles, but in comparison to the wars being fought in Africa and Asia, nothing that occurred during the "Black Wars" rises to anything that might be considered a major conflict. In most cases, they were simply massacres that ended up being recorded.

The first white settlements were along the banks of the Hawkesbury River, leading inland from the river mouth located a few miles up the coast from Sydney. The region was heavily populated by Aboriginal people belonging to the Darug group, a coastal foraging people whose language encompassed an area of about 2,300 square miles around Port Jackson and Botany Bay. What followed is now known as the "Hawkesbury and Nepean Wars," which, from about 1795-1816, comprised Aboriginal raids on farms and the reprisals that these provoked. In 1816, Governor Macquarie deployed a detachment of the 46th Regiment of Foot to patrol the populated reaches of the Hawkesbury River, ending in a raid on an encampment that claimed the lives of 14

Aboriginals.

Similar attacks and raids in and around Parramatta were dealt with by an official sanction, made by Governor Philip King, that Aboriginals could be legally shot on sight. This was not quite the bounty offered in Van Diemen's Land, but it placed the Aboriginals outside the protection of law, violating the essential element of the British imperial charter. Apart from the occasional rumblings of concern from afar, no real effort was made by the British government to intervene. Typically, news of an event of significance did not reach Whitehall until a year later, and another year would pass before the official reprimand was read in Sydney, at which point no one really cared anymore. In a place where convicts were being routinely flogged to within an inch of their lives, the plight of some faceless band of Aboriginals being removed from the land hardly stirred national outrage.

The various coastal settlements encountered indigenous people in almost every instance, and in some cases the contact was friendly. One example can be found in the explorations of John Oxley, who anchored at Moreton Bay in 1823 on his way back from a visit to Port Curtis, both on the east coast of modern Queensland. There he found a shipwreck survivor who had lived among the Aborigines for years in a state of harmony. Likewise, there is the tale of William Buckley, who prospered for over 30 years among the Aborigines.

In fact, examples like those might have been the rule rather than the exception had the rapacious seizure of land for private use not characterized every step taken by the British as they moved deeper into the territory. Nowhere was this more pronounced than in Tasmania. Founded as a settlement in 1803, the temperate climate and fertility of the island saw it develop a vibrant settler culture alongside the establishment of a formal penal colony. Until the abolition of penal transportation in 1868, Van Diemen's Land, alongside Norfolk Island, served as the main penal complex, and it had become extremely sophisticated by the time the penal system was dissolved. At the same time, free settlers also trickled into Van Diemen's Land in steadily growing numbers, to the extent that when the Henty Brothers arrived in the mid-1830s, no spare arable land was available. In an environment such as this, the Aborigines simply had to go, and it was Governor George Arthur who pursued an extermination policy with the greatest vigor. This followed almost 25 years of attrition as indigenous people, numbering no more than a few thousand to begin with, mounted ever more determined resistance as white settlers increasingly laid claim to the land. This was a phase also known as the "Black War," and in its local context, it has often been cited as the most effective Aboriginal resistance of the era. White fatalities numbered some 50 individuals between 1828 and 1830, compelling many rural homesteads to be fortified. A shoot on sight policy was pursued under gubernatorial decree, and a heavy-handed application of capital punishment saw the gallows serve as a major weapon of war.

Matters came to a head in 1830 when Governor Arthur sought to bring about an end to the ongoing insecurity by implementing a massive sweep across the island, known as the "Black

Line." Every able-bodied male in the colony joined, including convicts, and as dwindling bands of Aborigines were flushed out and killed, resistance effectively collapsed. A broken and diminished society of indigenous Tasmanians was gathered together and exiled on Flinders Island, located to the northeast of Van Diemen's Land, where a reservation was founded under a degree of government administration.

A similar state of affairs took place on the Bathurst Plain as soon as white settlers began crossing the Blue Mountains and parceling up land for the establishment of farms. This was land occupied by the Wiradjuri people, more numerous and more aggressive in general than the Darug. Aggressive Aboriginal attacks were regularly launched against isolated homesteads, often accompanied by larceny, and these were almost always followed up by a bloody reprisal attack. Frontier law prevailed, and frontier justice was liberally applied.

In 1824, Governor Brisbane placed the settled region surrounding Bathurst under martial law, for reasons, he said, "[to end] the Slaughter of Black Women and Children, and unoffending White Men." It might also be interesting to note that it was Brisbane who established the New South Wales Mounted Police as a paramilitary protection force and an agent of law enforcement.[5] The force was initially deployed against bushrangers, another source of insecurity on the frontier, and an inevitable byproduct of such a remote penal settlement.[6]

This, then, was the state of things as the colony and its various settlements slowly took root across Australia, and the dispersed aboriginal community had to digest the bitter threat that this represented to their society and way of life. As further colonies were added to the evolving commonwealth, the violent dispossession of indigenous people accelerated. Matters would not be taken up by a native affairs administration in any meaningful way until the early 1960s, and prior to that, moral responsibility for Aboriginal protection and well-being lay largely with Christian missionaries.

On October 18, 1928, the last recorded act of the Frontier Wars took place in what was known as the "Coniston Massacre." In August of that year, a dingo hunter by the name of Frederick Brooks was killed by Aborigines, and over the course of the next several months, according to the official record, 31 Aborigines were hunted down and killed. Historians, however, suggest that the number was much higher, perhaps as high as 110 men, women and children.

That said, by the mid-19th century, the Frontier Wars amounted to little more than mopping up the exhausted natives, many of whom were debilitated by disease. Aboriginal numbers were critically reduced, and the natives were capable of little more than occasional bouts of banditry.

---

[5] The New South Wales Mounted Police remains part of the New South Wales Police Force. It was founded on 7 September 1825, recruited from a British military regiment stationed in NSW at the time. Its mandate was to protect travellers, suppress convict escapees and fight indigenous Australians.

[6] *Bushrangers* were in the main escaped convicts adopting a life as outlaws and relying on robbery for survival. The most famous of these was Ned Kelly.

By then, many Aboriginals were also relinquishing their traditional occupation of the land, entering employment, urbanizing and submitting to education and modern life. The Aboriginal and indigenous Torres Strait Island population is estimated to have been in the region of 800,000 at the time of the occupation, yet it had fallen to a low in 1900 of about 117,000, a decrease of about 85%.

The Musket Wars

"There is not a bay, not a cove in New Zealand which has not witnessed horrible dramas, and woe to the white man who falls into the New Zealanders' hands." - Dr Felix Maynard and Alexandre Dumas

The Musket Wars define a lengthy episode of Māori history that is as unique as it was tragic. The simple dynamic of the Musket Wars was the sudden acquisition by various groups and individuals of ballistic weapons. This, in a society, balanced and configured by war, and the iconography of war, was nothing less than a seminal moment. All of the elements of Māori society – the political divisions, the circulating cause and effect of mana and utu and a tradition of internecine warfare – provided the basic alchemy of total war, once the ingredient of firearms was added. It has often been remarked that Native American and Aboriginal societies were decimated by introduced diseases, but it was introduced technology that began the Māori decline.

Again, one must be wary of oversimplification, for introduced diseases also affected large portions of the Māori population, and modern historians have tended to downplay the practical impact of traded muskets on Māori warfare since they were uniformly of low quality and unreliable manufacture. At the same time, some made better use of this technology than others.

What is undeniable, however, was that the introduction of ballistics, primitive and inefficient as they may have been, radically altered the face of intertribal warfare in New Zealand, devastating some tribes and radically altering traditional territorial boundaries. Across the land, guns terminally disrupted the established social order.

The first substantive contact between Europeans and Māoris began with the arrival of whalers and fur seal hunters, who began to appear off the coast of New Zealand within a few years of James Cook's final visit. At the hands of these early visitors, the first superficial trade between the white man and Māori began. Initially, this trade was in iron implements and tools, clothing and other oddments of modern manufacture. It was in the development of the flax and timber trade, however, at the hands of Sydney based merchants, that firearms began to be traded. Initially, these were basic trade guns, manufactured for the West African trade and of extremely dubious quality and utility. Nonetheless, these began to be used as trade items for timber rights, and the direct purchase of flax, which the Māori grew. At the moment that the Māori began to appreciate the martial potential of these weapons, the Musket Wars began.

The man most widely credited with triggering the Musket Wars is the Ngāpuhi chief Hongi Hika. The Ngāpuhi were a Māori iwi located in the region of the Northland Peninsula at the extreme north of North Island. Hongi Hika was the first to acquire muskets in any numbers, and he used them in the Battle of Moremonui, fought at Maunganui Bluff, Northland either in 1807 or 1808. The Ngāpuhi's opponents in this battle were the neighboring Ngāti Whātua, who were not armed with muskets but still got the better of the engagement as Hongi Hika and his men fumbled with the unfamiliar mechanisms of their muskets and failed to deliver any firepower. It was a humiliating defeat, mana was disrupted, and utu demanded revenge.

A sketch of Hongi Hika

Hongi Hika was no fool, and he realized very quickly that the primary advantage in having ballistic weapons lay in the shock and awe produced on those unfamiliar with them. In short order, Hongi Hika won his revenge and then began raiding southwards for slaves because guns were expensive and slaves were needed to cultivate the potatoes and flax. They produced as much food as they could sell to buy more weapons, so as guns flooded into certain regions, hunger among the common people often accompanied them.

In 1820, Hongi Hika, in the company of the Church Missionary Society missionary Thomas Kendall, visited England, ostensibly in order to assist in the production of a Māori dictionary. However, Hongi Hika was more interested in the guns that he had heard were stored in the

Tower of London. While in England, he was introduced to King George IV and was lavished with gifts, including a full suit of armor. He was unable to gain any access to the arsenal in the Tower of London, but upon arriving in Sydney on the way home, he exchanged his haul of gifts for some 300 muskets, keeping only a coat of mail, which saved his life more than once in battle and enhanced his mana as an invincible warrior.

Those 300 muskets ultimately tipped the balance, giving Hongi Hika and his army an assailable edge. This prompted an arms race as other powerful chiefs rushed to equalize their position, or at least retain the ability to mount a credible defense. The first to do so were the Bay of Islands communities, and once a certain equilibrium had been established, the heavily armed tribes of the north turned on the tribes of the south that had not yet begun to arm. The panic caused by the initial shock of these attacks secured numerous decisive victories for the Ngāpuhi. Tribes under threat of attack, however, scurried to acquire stocks of this new weapon, and soon various campaigns were underway across the region as weaker tribes fell upon each other.

The Musket Wars lasted on paper from 1807-1842, comprising numerous battles and campaigns on both islands. Suddenly, from a handful of obsolete muskets appearing here and there in the order of battle, there was an orchestrated use of ballistic weapons, aided on occasions by artillery pieces and the adaption of tactics and strategies. As the trade in muskets developed, and better supplies were established, Māori musketeers were better placed to train and thus develop appropriate strategies. At the same time, traditional Māori warfare tended to be ritualized, and on numerous occasions the warring groups were linked by ties of kinship, so debilitating death tolls were certainly not desirable. The ultimate objective of all war was to defeat the strongest tribe, so in a sense, Māori warfare can be seen in the context of a sports tournament, thus resuming every fighting season.

Traditional Māori tactics of warfare were organized and relatively sophisticated, but the ritualization ensured that the fighting was not done in the most efficient manner, at least from modern perspectives. The movement of manpower was often in large and ritualized war canoes, and speed and surprise were the essence of offensive strategy. Individual combat was also governed by rules of ritual and tradition, to the point that the Māori haka is perhaps one of the most elaborate and theatrical preambles to war ever devised. Traditional weaponry, notwithstanding wide regional variation, and highly specific functions and significance, can be defined basically as spears and clubs. No shields were used, so a wooden-bladed spear, used either as a javelin or a lance, held an enemy at bay while the club was wielded to try and get in a killing strike.

Even Māori cannibalism was ritualistic, with the fundamental correlation of eating an enemy, or parts thereof to assimilate the dead warrior's power and mana. Peace, if such a thing was ever realistically sought, was almost never achieved in battle. Battle and war were means unto themselves, and the higher result was always brokered through marriages and alliances. Even then, marriages and alliances were geared towards a better performance in the field.

All of this, of course, was drastically altered by the introduction of firearms. Māori tactics of warfare relegated clubs and spears to rear echelon infantry while controlled volleys and skirmishing characterized the action at the front. The Māori, with a finely tuned instinct for combat, adapted to the musket as a weapon of war extremely well, and instinctively understood the appropriate tactics. Concepts such as supporting fire, controlled fire, skirmishing, and breastworks seemed to come naturally. Battlements and fortified pā were further adapted as a defense against gunfire. Campaigning was also now conducted on very different terms, and on a different scale. Full blown invasions became frequent, significant boundary shifts began to affect long-established patterns of ownership, and ancient power balances changed or were obliterated.

There were other social changes that helped facilitate an entirely different view of warfare. The traditional role of men, for example, was as cultivators and warriors, and the cultivation of traditional crops was governed strictly by established rituals and tapu. Time spent engaged in warfare, therefore, was dictated somewhat by the necessity to cultivate and work the land. Campaigns were also moderated by logistics, mainly in terms of food, and how far a war party could travel away from its support base. All of this changed with the introduction by Europeans of potatoes. The Musket Wars have often been called the "Potato Wars" for precisely this reason, because the changes brought about by potatoes were probably no less radical than firearms. Potatoes were a non-traditional Māori food crop, and they revolutionized domestic production. In the first instance, they provided for an almost immediate food surplus, which was traded, alongside an increased production of pigs, for yet more guns. Just as importantly, potatoes proved to be the ideal campaign food, which in turn made it possible to conduct far more wide-ranging campaigns. Best of all, potatoes did not demand ritualized cultivation by men, which changed the essential pattern of domestic production. Food could now be cultivated by women and slaves, liberating men to apply themselves more exclusively to warfare.

The weight of all of these changes on traditional society was enormous. The cost of a single musket in 1820 was about 200 baskets of potatoes or 15 pigs, and although prices fluctuated and lowered over time, it was still a heavy price. 200 baskets of potatoes and 15 pigs might sustain an average family for a year, perhaps more, so for the sake of a single rifle, the resources of an entire community would need to be mobilized for at least that period. In the perverse logic of war, it was not infrequent for communities to go hungry despite this surplus so that a warrior or two could be armed and supplied with powder and shot.

After the initial successes of the Ngāpuhi, the emphasis tended to be a shifting alliance of northern tribes moving progressively against the weaker tribes in the south of North Island. Hongi Hika, however, was killed in March 1828, dying from injuries sustained by a musket shot. His death marked the beginning of the end of Ngāpuhi predominance, and by the early 1830s, they had more or less disappeared from the picture. His position was assumed by a lesser known, but generally more respected fighting commander by the name of Te Rauparaha, of the Ngāti Toa iwi. Known as the Napoleon of the South, more biographies have been written about Te Rauparaha than any other New Zealander.

As ballistic weapons began to find their way into the hands of northern tribes, the Ngāti Toa were among the first to acquire them. An early alliance between the Ngāti Toa and the Ngāpuhi, sometime in 1819, saw a large war party on a sustained series of campaigns that penetrated south as far as Cook Strait. However, instability and insecurity in and around their original home of Kāwhia, on the west coast of the Northern Peninsula, had the effect of pushing the Ngāti Toa progressively southwards, and they entered upon a period of their history known as "The Migration." This was, in essence, an ongoing rearguard action as the Ngāti Toa fought the stronger tribes of the north and were pushed out. However, while they were being pushed back, they were subjugating smaller local tribes in the south, who subsequently fell upon others. A circulating pattern of conquest began, and it continued for some time, ending around the early 1830s with the Ngāti Toa dominating the southern quarter of North Island. They established themselves on Kapiti Island, a few miles offshore of the southwest coast of North Island. This was an almost impenetrable position that remained the Ngāti Toa headquarters until peace returned.

Te Rauparaha emerged as one of the most influential and iconic figures of the Musket Wars, surviving to lead his nation in the next phase of war, the "New Zealand Wars." However, by the end of the 1830s, things were beginning to settle down, and the Musket Wars were effectively over. By then, British administration had begun to take effect, and white settlements expanded to exert their own influence on the countryside. The radical changes that had taken place in Māori society during the period of the Musket Wars, in particular in terms of land occupation and ownership, were codified under the law by a Native Land Court, established by the new colonial government to deal with issues of land as they related to the Māori. This established Māori communal land rights accordingly, notwithstanding how the traditional map may have looked a generation earlier. The emphasis, of course, was not on protecting indigenous land rights, but alienating land for whites' use. Exhausted by decades of war, the Māori largely submitted to the changes. By then, a small but robust settlement had taken root in the Bay of Islands, and satellite communities and settlements were springing up all over the territory. It was now generally appreciated by the new colonial administration, such as it was, that some sort of overarching agreement or treaty between the British authorities and the Māori was inevitable, and its purpose was to legalize British annexation, was inevitable.

The style of white settlement until then had been rather haphazard, with independent settlements taking root on the basis of timber extraction, whaling, or seal hunting. Though mostly impermanent, they nonetheless represented the first inroads of organized settlement in some of the most remote places. Things, however, were about to change, because in England, a Royal Chartered Company, the New Zealand Company, was hard at work trying to organize an assisted immigration program to bring over shiploads of English immigrants to take up the commercial tenure of land. Anxious to gain squatter rights before the formal British annexation of the territory, the New Zealand Company would launch an aggressive series of survey expeditions that triggered a new round of war.

Te Rauparaha

The New Zealand Wars

"The British soldier found the Māori warrior the grandest native enemy that he had ever encountered. Gurkhas and Sikhs were formidable before them: Zulus were formidable after them, but all these had copied European discipline. Tha Māori had his own code of war, the essence of which was a fair fight on a day and place fixed by appointment." – Sir John Forescue

For a long time, New Zealand was regarded purely as a commercial resource of New South Wales, and most of the early economic activity that increasingly introduced permanent settlement to the islands originated in New South Wales. It was merchants from Sydney, and later Hobart who pioneered the flax, timber, fur seal and whaling industries, and Sydney was the base from which the first Christian missions found their way to New Zealand.

The first recorded permanent settlement was in Dusky Sound, in 1792, located amongst the beautiful fjords of South Island. This was an insubstantial settlement that did not survive long. The 1825 settlement of Codfish Island, to the northwest of Stewart Island, in the extreme south of South Island, lasted a little longer, but it was soon shifted across the strait to Stewart Island, and then on to the mainland. These were all sealing and whaling depots, without any particular pretense at permanence. Those that began the exploit the timber reserves of the islands, concentrated mostly along the windward slopes of South Island, and in pockets of North Island, became the first of what might be regarded as permanent settlements. The timber of the region offered up a very necessary resource in the age of wooden ships, and once discovered, an organized timber industry, centered in Sydney, quickly kicked into gear. By 1816, the first cargoes of timber sawn and processed in New Zealand by permanently settled sawyers began to arrive in Sydney.

A census conducted in 1836 revealed that fully a third of all permanently settled European males in New Zealand were engaged in timber processing and export. Shore-based whaling operations were established soon afterwards, mainly along the east coast from Foveaux Strait, at the southern tip of South Island, to East Cape, the eastern-most point of North Island. By 1830, or thereabouts, some 15 Sydney based firms and companies were managing twenty-two separate whaling settlements within this region. Some of these were quite substantial, for example in the Bay of Plenty, but others were sparsely populated and transitory.

The demographic was mixed, with many Māori engaged, and a steady interaction between settler men and Māori women occurred, with the inevitable result. Convicts, army and navy deserters and many others made up a population mainly of men, somewhat predisposed to violence and crime, and inclined towards dissolute habits. Fugitive convicts from the penal settlements of Australia were recorded in the Bay of Islands as early 1815, a fact observed by Charles Darwin when he visited the site in 1835. In 1837, the *Sydney Herald* estimated a population of between 200 and 300 escaped convicts in New Zealand, mainly in the Bay of Islands.

Among these were a group known as the *Pākehā Māori*, from the word Pākehā, the general Māori term for a white or European person. The Pākehā Māori were simply white men forced for one reason or another to take refuge in Māori communities, beyond the reach of British justice. One can assume, therefore, that most of these were escaped convicts and general fugitives although there certainly were those who entered that life as a matter of preference and were content within it. In rare instances, whites were held by the Māori as slaves although this certainly was rare. The number of Pākehā Māori in 1830 was about fifty, and a decade later about 150. Most were either English or Irish, and a majority appear to have rejoined white society more or less as British sovereignty was declared.

The missionaries, of course, represented another demographic, and the first permanent missionaries arrived as part of the Church Missionary Society initiative, led by the Reverend Samuel Marsden in 1814. Many of the dispersed mission stations that were seeded from the initial settlement in the Bay of Islands became the basis of later towns and cities. On the eve of British sovereignty in 1840, Church and Wesleyan Missionary Society missionaries, and their families, numbered 206.

Then there were the free settlers, a sporadic addition to the commercial and missionary populations, and again mostly drifting across from New South Wales and other Australian settlements. The pace of free immigration began to quicken as the date of British annexation neared. This was partly because the establishment of a British colony required not only the recruitment of administrative personnel to take up various functions of government and the judiciary, but also because the development of a capital and the various construction and building projects associated with this further demanded the importation of skilled labor, many of whom brought their families. It is also true that land occupied prior to annexation was generally regarded as a *fait accompli*, so there were many attempting to gain land before a British administration could be introduced on the islands.

All of this also happened to coincide with the drought in New South Wales, the steady increase in the price of land and diminishing scope for settlement. The Swan River Settlement in Western Australia, a bold experiment in systematic settlement, had fared poorly, and a number of disappointed colonists from this region eventually made their way to New Zealand. New Zealand offered a new land with fresh opportunities, and as the century progressed, many people were alerted to this.

Settlements were already beginning to form at Wellington and Nelson, in the Cook Strait, and recognizing in due course that the former offered a more central location for the administration of both islands, the territorial capital was moved to Wellington in 1865.

The attributes of New Zealand as a destination for British emigration were by the first decades of the 19th century well appreciated. The islands, in particular North Island, enjoyed a temperate climate suitable for European settlement, and fertile soils that were well drained and watered. Several attempts were made to organize systematic settlement, and although ultimately unsuccessful, they did succeed in introducing small numbers of fresh arrivals.

The first attempt was made in 1825, with the founding of the New Zealand Association, established in England to facilitate immigration to New Zealand, and to seek entry on a large scale into the flax, timber, whaling and fur industries. Somewhat as a by-product of this, organized immigration was also part of the New Zealand Association's plan. The New Zealand Association was superseded in 1825 by the New Zealand Company, which was not awarded its Royal Charter until 1841. At its founding, the Company unsuccessfully petitioned the British Imperial Government for a thirty-one-year period of exclusive trade, along with the right to settle the territory, and establish an army. Royal chartered companies were typically granted rights along these lines, examples of which, of course, are the Hudson Bay Company and the British East India Company. Trade in New Zealand was already dispersed quite widely by then, and a monopoly simply would not have been possible. The use of private armies, along the lines of the Indian Army, was not an attractive idea in New Zealand, because war would have been inevitable, and the British Imperial Government would have been required inevitably to intercede.

Nevertheless, the following year, the New Zealand Company dispatched two ships, the *Lambton* and the *Isabella*, under the command of Captain James Herd, to examine trade prospects and identify potential settlements. Sometime in September or October of 1826, the two ships dropped anchor in the Cook Straits, in present day Wellington Harbor which was very quickly established as a suitable site for permanent settlement. A million acres of land was supposedly purchased from the Māori although no documentation to this effect is in existence, and certainly nothing came of it.

The next venture of this kind, also underwritten by the New Zealand Company, was the voyage of the ship *Tory*, which anchored in Port Nicholson in August 1939, also with a view to identifying and purchasing likely sites for organized settlement. The first immigrant ship, the *Aurora*, of which we have already heard, arrived in Wellington Harbor in January 1840. Named after the Duke of Wellington, the proposed settlement was part of the New Zealand Companies model of organized colonization. This model, incidentally, was conceived and developed by Edward Gibbon Wakefield, a colorful character who was involved in quite a number of similar schemes in Australia and Canada before his engagement with the New Zealand Company.

Again, part of the haste in reforming the New Zealand Company, and then attempting to establish settlements in New Zealand had to do with pending British Imperial plans to establish a crown colony in New Zealand, after which the freebooting acquisition of land would be impossible. Wakefield, by then a forty-three-year-old adventurer with a highly checkered past, was invited to join the Company as a director. His philosophy was simple: "Possess yourself of the Soil and you are Secure."[7] The Wakefield Plan envisaged packages of land comprising a "town acre," accompanied by 100 country acres, and 1,100 such one-acre town sections were planned for Port Nicholson. This, then, became the basis for the settlement and establishment of Wellington,

From 1835-1840, the Colonial Office dithered over precisely what to do with New Zealand. In the spring of 1836, the Governor of New South Wales, Sir Richard Bourke, dispatched a naval expedition under the command of Captain William Hobson to visit New Zealand in order to investigate firsthand the situation in the territory. Hobson's recommendation was simply that

---

[7] Edward Gibbon Wakefield was perhaps most widely known for an episode known as the "Shrigley Abduction," during which he abducted a fifteen-year-old heiress and forced her to marry him, for which he and his brother received a three-year prison sentence.

British sovereignty be declared over limited areas of British and European settlement, with a view then to an incremental increase in claims over the entire territory. This report was forwarded to the Colonial Office for consideration, and in the spring of 1838, a House of Lords Select Committee met to consider the "State of the Islands of New Zealand." Submissions were made by various bodies, including private, public, commercial, and religious interests. This resulted in Letters Patent issued to expand the territorial scope of New South Wales to include both the North and South Islands of New Zealand in their entirety. The Governor of New South Wales, then Sir George Gipps, was formally given the additional responsibility of Governor of New Zealand.

Hobson

This, then, was the first clear statement of intent on the part of the British Imperial Government that it intended to make a formal claim over New Zealand. Prior to this, Hobson's suggestion of limited British sovereignty was weighed up, and although very nearly reaching a consensus, did not quite. The idea as it was discussed in Whitehall was simply for a "Māori State," perhaps even a republic, within which British settlers were guaranteed certain rights of land and representation. In the end, a full settler state was agreed to, and in practical terms, the declaration of independence was immediately rendered moot.

Hobson was then appointed British Consul to New Zealand, and to him fell the task of establishing the constitutional framework of a new colony, and also of negotiating the surrender of Māori sovereignty to the British Crown. Under instructions from the Home Secretary, the Marquis of Normanby, Hobson was to "seek a cession of sovereignty, to assume complete control over land matters, and to establish a form of civil government." No draft treaty was given to him to work with, however, so he was left largely to his own resources to create the necessary instruments.

The official British position, as these steps were being taken, was ostensibly to protect Māori interests. This idea lay very much at the fore of the imperial establishment at the time. The traditional view of the British Empire is that it was a rapacious, exploitative and violent institution that left the destroyed remains of native society in its wake. This was more the attitude of the settler communities themselves, and quite often the Imperial Government was at odds with overseas colonies over precisely this question. In 1837, for example, a British Parliamentary Select Committee sat to examine the state and condition of all aboriginal subjects of Her Majesty. The Committee met "to consider what measures ought to be adopted with regards to the native inhabitants of the countries where British settlements are made, and to the neighboring tribes, in order to secure to them the due observance of justice, and the protection of their rights; to promote the spread of civilization among them, and to lead them to the peaceful and voluntary reception of the Christian religion."

This was something of a clarion call to missionaries and administrators across the British Empire to pay greater heed to the effects that European settlements were having on the native races of the world. This concern was expressed largely for the natives of North America, the Hottentot of the Cape, and the Aborigines of Australia. The Māori were not held to be in quite the same class as these, and they were not regarded as imperiled in any way, but nonetheless, it was a sensitive issue, and the Imperial Government felt the need to tread warily.

By 1839, Te Rauparaha and the Ngāti Toa were headquartered on Kapiti Island, just off the southern coast of North Island. On October 16, a small expedition of white men, commanded by Colonel William Wakefield, arrived and requested the purchase of land for white settlers. Te Rauparaha obliged, and this formed the basis of the settlement of Nelson, on the north coast of South Island, and the bays that are today known as Tasman and Golden.

Then, a few months later, word reached Te Rauparaha through the missionary, Reverend Henry Williams, that all Māori chiefs were to be summoned to Kororāreka by the British consul William Hobson for a grand council. This was the preamble to the Treaty of Waitangi,

On January 29, 1840 William Hobson arrived in the Bay of Islands, with a ship of the recently chartered New Zealand Company, the *Cuba*, arriving not far behind. This ship carried Company members commissioned to conduct a survey on the feasibility of organized settlement, and to break ground prior to the arrival of shiploads of assisted immigrants. Already anchored in the harbor was the *Aurora*, carrying the first of these Company settlers. The New Zealand Company was anxious to get all of this done and to take up land before British annexation and the complications that would follow.

The next day was a Thursday, and Hobson wasted no time in calling a general meeting at Christs Church at Kororāreka. By presenting the Letters Patent of 1839, he announced the establishment of British sovereignty, confirmed his own appointment and let it be known that a process of establishing the constitutional basis of the new colony would commence immediately.

The basis of any style of colony could only be consequent to some sort of agreement by treaty with the various Māori iwi. This was clearly understood by all parties, and it cannot therefore be said that the Māori were duped into anything or negotiated with in bad faith. In general, the Māori were respectful of the British at that time. Many Māori served as crewmembers on British ships and thus traveled, with quite a number visiting England. As a result, they had a much clearer sense of the world than many other native peoples at that time. The British were a great maritime and trading nation, and the benefits and ramifications of a grand alliance with them were reasonably understood.

The treaty that followed was carefully drafted and amended by Hobson himself, assisted by Busby as official Resident and Hobson's private secretary James Freeman. None of these men were lawyers, however, so the basic structure of the treaty was borrowed from the text of various preexisting British treaties. It was ready for translation in just four days. From there it was handed over to the missionary Henry Williams, who, along with his son, was fluent in *Te Reo,* the lingua franca of the Māori. It was they who constructed the Māori version of the document. This was done overnight, and on February 5, 1840 it was ready for circulation among the various Māori chiefs.

Williams

In a single sentence of 216 words, Hobson introduced himself as a constituted functionary of Her Majesty Victoria, with powers to establish government, and to control and manage European settlement, both current and pending, and empowered moreover to treat with the Māori. Thereafter, as contained in three articles, all sovereignty was to be ceded to the British Crown, the Māori were guaranteed continued, undisturbed access to their lands and resources, the Crown reserved first right of preemption for any land alienated, and the Māori were guaranteed of all the rights and privileges owed to any other British subjects.

The translation of this document was inevitably imperfect, and in the years since, it has been examined minutely for any evidence of deliberate duplicity, but the findings in general have tended to suggest not. The English and Māori versions of the treaty document are substantially the same, except for one or two subtle differences that might bear accusations of intentional ambiguity. In fact, the difficulty that Henry Williams encountered was in the absence of appropriate Māori language to cover some of the concepts imparted. For example, in Article One, the English version stated that the chiefs were obliged to cede all rights and powers of sovereignty to the Crown, while in the Māori version, the implication is quite different. Here it states that Māori chiefs relinquish all "government" to the Crown, which, of course, implies

Crown responsibility for administration and not full and sovereign overlordship. No direct translation for "sovereignty" exists in Māori, simply because the Māori functioned on the level of individual tribes without any paramount ruler. In a second point, the jumbled and rather chaotic interpretation seems not to have conveyed clearly the concept of "preemption," and the question of land and land purchase as a whole.[8]

Nonetheless, it was this document that was presented to an assembly of northern chiefs inside an expansive marquee erected on the grounds of Busby's home in Waitangi. The document was read aloud, first in English by Hobson, and then in *Te Reo* by Henry Williams. Thereafter, for some five hours, the contents of the draft treaty were debated by the Māori chiefs, and most accounts of the episode tend to portray it as a fractious and angry interlude, with subtle divisions that were not easy for the whites to interpret. There was, for example, division between converted Catholic and Anglican members of the Māori leadership, and this was in part because the small Catholic mission fraternity, mainly French, but also Irish, had been at work urging the chiefs not to trust the British authorities. There was a general resistance to the notion of a "Governor," and the loss of land, and in some instances it was demanded that land already purchased or occupied be returned. That said, the arguments seemed to be formulaic and rather spurious in character, for when the time came to ratify the treaty, 45 chiefs of North Island, representing the majority, presented themselves to sign. In fact, they arrived a day early, on February 6, which forced Hobson to improvise a ceremony.

In the end, it would seem that a rather sophisticated interpretation of the situation convinced the chiefs that the likely benefits of British sovereignty and protection would outweigh the disadvantages. It is also true that those gathering to debate the matter understood quite clearly the international dynamic now at play. If the British were denied constitutional sovereignty by treaty, then they would achieve it in some other way, probably by conquest, and the terms might then not be so generous. Moreover, there were always the French, occupying Polynesian islands where and when they could. Given a chance, they would certainly make a play for New Zealand, and in the grand scheme of things, the British were preferred.

Thus, on February 6, 1840, the "Treaty of Waitangi" was signed, and Busby's home thus acquired the name "Treaty House." Further signatures were later added, and on May 21, 1840, sovereignty was declared over North Island on the basis of the Waitangi Treaty, and over South Island by virtue of prior discovery by Captain James Cook in 1769.

Throughout the course of European imperial history, a great deal of issues arose over treaty translations. In the Māori translation of this document, the concept of "full rights and powers of sovereignty" reads more along the line of general administrative authority, or government, and not a replacement power for the "confederated tribes." Moreover, with regard to the elemental

---

[8] "Preemption" is described by the Oxford Dictionary as the purchase of goods or shares by one person or party before the opportunity is offered to others.

point of land, "full exclusive and undisturbed possession" read more as "sovereignty," or "chieftainship." From this, it is not difficult to extrapolate an understanding that the British would administer the affairs of the nation in the wider, global context, but that this would not in any way alter the traditional institutions of power and authority. In fact, the clause of preemption gave the British government first right of purchase of any native land, which was what the likes of the New Zealand Company had feared because effective control of the land was ceded to the British authorities since no sale or transfer could take effect without its permission.

The aftermath all but assured war, and the first shots were fired almost before the ink of the Treaty of Waitangi was dry. If a confederation of Māori tribes in peace was unlikely, in war it was somewhat more probable, and in the face of a common enemy, common cause motivated the Māori probably for the first time in their history.

The New Zealand Wars lasted on paper from 1845-1872, and in many respects it was like a traditional British colonial war, a war of pacification no different than the kind fought in India and South Africa. The first exchange of fire between the British and Māori occurred during what was known as the "Wairau Affray," which was consequent to the sale of land to agents of the New Zealand Company by Te Rauparaha and the Ngāti Toa. There are no specific details on the area of land included in this sale; in fact, William Wakefield never dealt directly with Te Rauparaha but instead made the purchase through a third party, a whaling captain named John Blenkinsopp who claimed to have purchased it directly from Te Rauparaha. The New Zealand Company agents, therefore, who then set off in 1843 to act upon the purchase, did so based on a fraudulent sale that had no particular basis under law. Captain Arthur Wakefield, William Wakefield's younger brother, remarked in a letter to the Company as he surveyed the prospects, "I rather anticipate some difficulty with the natives."

The Company established the settlement of Nelson in Tasman Bay on the south shore of Cook Strait. On the surface, this might have seemed an ideal location, and from the point of view of coastal and port facilities, it was. It did not, however, take long for it to become evident that arable land was limited, and the hinterland was blocked in by hills and mountains. Survey parties then began to probe north and south until the wide and fertile valley of the Wairau River was discovered. This immediately excited the interest of the Company, and surveying began in haste. Naturally, the local Māori observed with alarm the busy investigations of a growing corps of armed white men, and in January 1843, Te Rauparaha sent his older brother Nohorua at the head of a delegation of chiefs to Nelson. There a formal protest was lodged against British activity in the Wairau Plains. When this had no effect, Te Rauparaha himself appeared, urging that land delineations and purchases be left to the arbitration of the Native Land Commission, then at work with a commission in Wellington.

The Company was certainly not going to do that, and when the commission inevitably caught up with it, it wished to be in full possession of any lands claimed. Arthur Wakefield offered payment for the land it intended to settle, and when this was refused, an attempt was made to arrest Te Rauparaha. This sparked a battle in which 22 whites were killed; quite a few of whom were executed after they were captured. Needless to say, those executions were anything but humane.

The incident was a setback to New Zealand Company ambitions, and the activities of the Company proved not to be particularly successful in the long term. The Wairau Affray, however, was the first incident of what was known at the time as the Māori Wars, and later the New Zealand Wars, and the only one to take place on South Island.

The scene of the Wairau Affray

The next substantive phase of the war began in the north, around the Bay of Islands, and is known as the "Flagstaff War," after rebellious Māori hacked down the flagstaff above the settlement of Kororāreka. This symbol of insurrection sparked a series of conflicts that spilled over into 1846, spreading between 1846 and 1847 to the south of North Island, and in the hinterland of Wellington. From this rose a movement known as the Kīngitanga, or "Māori King Movement," which attempted to revive the role of Māori traditional leadership, and under whose broad aegis the various battles and campaigns were fought.

Some of the heaviest fighting took place in the 1860s and early 1870s, with notable actions fought at Taranaki, Waikato, and the Bay of Plenty between 1860 and 1864. Thereafter, between 1864 and 1872, British operations were confined to suppressing the last flares of resistance here and there and mopping up rebellious pockets. At its peak, the colonial government fielded a force numbering some 18,000 men, against a peak Māori force of about 5,000. The spirit of resistance, however, was broken, and the last holdouts tended to be bands of fanatical guerrillas led by prophetic leaders, determined to hold out to the last.

Ultimately, the New Zealand Wars marked the end of independent Māori rule. If the Musket Wars weakened traditional Māori society, the New Zealand Wars broke it entirely.

Land Confiscations

"AND WHEREAS … Her Majesty may be pleased to waive in favor of the Natives so much of the said Treaty of Waitangi as reserves to Her Majesty the right of pre-emption of their lands…"
- The Native Land Act 1862

The New Zealand Wars ended in a Māori "defeat," a term that does not entirely do justice to what happened. Some 700 years of Māori independent history ended, and New Zealand became a British colony unencumbered by dispute or disunity. At the same time, the attributes of New Zealand as a destination for large-scale British settlement were well appreciated, and immigrants were flooding into the colony. Land then became the currency of expansion, and since they were defeated in battle, by the laws of conquest, the Māori ceded title to their land. None of it was quite so cut and dried as this, of course, but almost at the moment that the New Zealand Wars ended, land confiscations began.

In 1865, a Native Land Act was passed that created a Native Land Court intended to arbitrate in order to avoid any repeat of incidences like the Wairau Affray. There were numerous provisions to the act, one being that no more than 10 people might be named on a single title, which was intended to break the pattern of communal land ownership at the heart of the Māori understanding of land and ownership. It also required that Māori ownership be proven, and that any land claimed by a Māori be surveyed and lodged, all of which cost money and required a relatively sophisticated understanding of modern procedure and law. After title was decided, land then became available for sale, and many individuals or groups of Māori did indeed sell their land.

Land confiscations were another story altogether, and a rather different strategy with strong punitive overtones. The idea was originally suggested by the New Zealand Premier to the British Governor in the early 1860s, and it certainly was nothing new across the empire. In many parts of the world, the British colonizing authorities confiscated native land as punishment for rebellions, most notably in Ireland, and this was in essence what was proposed here. An additional advantage, of course, over and above stamping the authority of the British Crown, was the availability of large amounts of fresh land for immigration and settlement. The legal basis for this course of action was contained in the New Zealand Settlements Act of 1863, which provided for the seizure of land from rebellious tribes after 1 January 1863. Confiscations

(Raupatu) under this Act took place in South Auckland, Waikato, Tauranga, Ōpōtiki–Whakatāne, Taranaki, and the Mōhaka–Waikare district in Hawke's Bay. There were also confiscations in Poverty Bay, but these were perpetrated under different legislation.

At first, it was assumed that these confiscations would be limited in scope and intended to foster peace and security by the settlement of military personnel and the marking out of towns and settlements. They soon grew more elaborate, however, with land taken from tribes that were loyal and disloyal to the Crown, and all under the guise of being for the good of the natives. Records of contemporary parliamentary debates and official correspondence point to a strong underlying motivation of accelerating and paying for increased colonization, and reducing the Māori to a point that they would never be able to challenge imperial rule again.

The Native Land Court, or Te Kōti Tango Whenua in Māori, was established purely to investigate Māori title to land, but the Native Lands Act of 1862, from which the legal basis of the Native Land Court was drawn, did, among other things, abolish the right to preemption.[9] It also created a framework by which communal title under customary law could be formalized to individual title, if that title could be proved. By 1872, the Native Land Court had issued titles to 5,013,839 acres of land, mostly in the provinces of Auckland, Wellington, and Hawke's Bay. This practically brought an end to the tradition of customary or communal title, which had always been a fly in the ointment of colonial land policy. It was, of course, not compulsory for the Māori to submit an application to the Native Land Court, and in theory they were free to continue under customary title if they chose. In practice, however, almost all land under Māori ownership came before the court in one way or another and was converted to freehold title. After 1865, very little land remained under customary title.

In 1873, a year after the conclusion of New Zealand Wars, and long after the dust had settled over most of the colony, a second Native Land Act was passed that abolished the "10 owner" rule and replaced it with a system whereby all owners of a block of land were entered into the court register. This created as many problems as it solved in the short term, but in the long term, it was a further step in the direction of formalizing and modernizing land ownership.

Perhaps not surprisingly, the net result of this process did not bring security of tenure for Māori individuals or communities. In many cases, Māori iwi were breaking up and falling under constitutional law, or migrating to the cities and entering formal labor. Free title to land simply made it available for sale, and although it also offered the opportunity to raise money and create a more viable income from land, in the end, most of it was sold off and was transferred from Māori to whites. Interestingly, the Crown remained the largest single purchaser of land in New Zealand - from 1870-1928, it acquired about 4 million hectares on North Island, while private purchases amounted to about 2 million.

---

[9] Te Kōti Tango Whenua meaning in direct translation "The Land Taking Court."

By the 20th century, very little land remained in Māori hands, so efforts were made to keep what did remain under Māori ownership intact, but they often failed. In 1900, the government passed the "Māori Land Administration Act," a bold effort driven largely by Māori politicians that did nothing to stem the outward flow of Māori land. During and after World War I, the government reentered the market and purchased significant amounts of land for distribution to returning veterans, and to attract more immigration among demobilized British servicemen.

Stolen Generations

When the British Parliamentary Select Committee was appointed to examine the circumstances and conditions of indigenous people in all of the British Overseas Territories in 1837, the phenomenon of British colonial expansion was gathering pace even as the abolition of slavery inspired a higher vision of the British Empire. It was clearer than ever that imperial Britain had inherited a specific responsibility for the millions of native peoples falling subject to the British Crown. This marked an important moment when the metropolitan authorities in England began to impose protections and limitations on the powers that settler communities could exercise over native populations. Some were more vulnerable than others, of course, but in general, colonization was proving calamitous to native communities all over the world. The Aboriginal people of Australia, who the British considered infinitely more primitive than natives in other regions, were clearly unable to stand up for themselves, and certainly not against a relentlessly aggressive colonial movement.

The Select Committee recommended, among other things, the appointment of a "Protector of Aborigines," which was the first step in a process that would replace the aggressive subjugation of a people with a smothering, overarching, and paternalistic management of their affairs.

Australia in the late 1830s remained a vast and wild land, and notwithstanding sentimental entreaties from London, it would be some time before the dust settled on the frontier. In 1869, the first formal legislation appeared on the Victoria Colony statute intended specifically to address Aboriginal rights and protections. The Aborigines Protection Act of 1869 made provision for the establishment of a Board for the Protection of Aborigines which granted extensive powers to a board of trustees who governed just about every aspect of Aborigine life. The same essential paternalism was taking root elsewhere in the colony, and elsewhere in the empire. Aboriginal Australians, however, were seen as particularly in need of protection, over and above Indian natives, who were regarded as civilized, or Africans, who had survived 300 years of slavery and were not about to succumb to pernicious disease or alcohol.

White Australians, in particular heavily religious Christians or those involved in government, saw the Aborigines as residing in the kindergarten of life, irresponsible to their own needs and clearly susceptible to vice. There was a growing interest in Victorian society to export the finer aspects of British society and assimilate natives in a way that would harmoniously establish a Christianized, Europeanized population fortified by Western morality and education, and thus equipped to step forth into the modern world. There was little chance that older adults would ever assimilate, so the idea of isolating Aboriginal youth from their indigenous families and lodging them instead in Christian missions and boarding schools began to take root.

There was nothing original about the idea of assimilating Aboriginal children by removing them from their native society; in fact, it was a policy commonly prescribed in many places at that time, and it would remain in vogue for almost a century. Around the same time, such policies were being applied to the native peoples of Alaska, Native Americans, and the Papuans. Given the racist roots at the heart of such a policy, it's ironic that Aboriginal "protection" as an idea was philanthropic in its origins, wrapped up in the growing reform movement in Britain, which saw social reforms take root in all directions. Just as the urban poor of industrial Britain deserved protection from exploitation and poverty, so did the Indians, the Africans, and the Aborigines. White, Christian, English speaking societies were viewed as the apex of mankind's cultural achievement, and to assimilate native peoples into that society was considered a gift. The idea is almost universally vilified today, and for good reasons, but the original concept was well-meaning in the sense that settlers were seeking a solution to a problem of their own making.

That the arrival of Europeans in Australia was catastrophic for the native race is hardly disputable, but once it became de facto, and once the sheer scale of the catastrophe became evident, some effort was demanded to repair the damage and protect the people affected from any further damage. The Aboriginal protection laws were a first step in this direction. The first thing that becomes apparent when reading the provisions of almost every law drafted for this purpose (and each of the Australian colonies produced their own version) is that Aboriginal people in their "wild" state were seen as fundamentally primitive, with no power or ability to govern their own lives in the context of a modern society. The Aboriginal protection laws, therefore, granted the various protectors of Aborigines almost universal authority, something akin to the power of a parent over a child. This offers perhaps the clearest indication of how Aborigines were viewed.

It is also perhaps worth noting that the policies that grew from the original drafting of the Victoria Aboriginal Protection Act are often regarded as genocide. This is a confusing idea because attempts to violently eradicate the indigenous people of the continent were a feature of early settlement and land conflicts, but genocide can have wider implications than simply that. To obliterate the cultural memory of an entire generation by removing it from the source of that culture and placing it instead within an alternative culture is widely regarded in modern times as a form of genocide.

Be that as it may, however, various Aboriginal Protection Boards came into being as the century progressed, each with a similar function. Ad hoc systems and processes had been underway almost since the onset of white settlement. The Port Philip "Protectorate" was established as a result of the 1837 Select Committee report, and in 1839, a Chief Protector of

Aborigines was appointed with assistants assigned to the various regions. The first school specifically to accommodate Aboriginal children was founded as early as 1814 by Governor Lachlan Macquarie, one of the more progressive and liberal governors of New South Wales. This was known as the "Native Institution" and functioned in various forms until 1830. The Public Instruction Act of 1880, in the meanwhile, legislated mandatory education for all children in New South Wales, including Aborigine children. Initially, a single integrated system was proposed, but in time a program of separate education came into effect. Three years later, the "Board for the Protection of Aborigines" was founded, and it managed to operate without statutory authority until 1909, when the "Aboriginal Protection Act" of that year was passed.

The 1909 Aboriginal Protection Act was in most ways a streamlining of older legislation, but it was the first to grant absolute legal authority to a board of trustees over all Aboriginal children. Prior to this, the board could only employ coercive strategies, such as stopping food rations to families whose children did not attend school. Children could, of course, also be removed from their families under general child welfare laws. The 1909 Act, however, offered a much wider scope for the management of Aborigines, albeit not absolute. Children could be removed from the care of their families if they were found by a magistrate to be "neglected," but part of the official definition of neglect was children with "no visible means of support or fixed place of abode." This obviously offered wide discretionary powers to any official, though a magistrate might still decline to declare a child neglected if he or she appeared to be well fed and clothed, even if the child lived in a traditional, nomadic Aboriginal encampment.

In 1915, after strenuous lobbying by the Aboriginal Protection Board, the Act was amended and stiffened, and at last the trustees were empowered to remove any child without parental consent if the Board considered it to be in the interest of the child's moral or physical welfare. It then became the responsibility of the parents to prove that the child in question was neither neglected nor at any particular risk. This stripped all parents of guardianship of their children and awarded the Board almost unlimited power, power that was also wielded by the white management and administration of Aborigine stations, as well as police authorities in the Aboriginal reserves.

These various authorities were now also empowered to remove much younger children, and in 1916, the Board began taking children under the terms of the 1915 amendments. It is interesting to note that white children could also suffer removal under general child welfare legislation, and for the same essential reasons, but usually they were allowed to retain contact with their families by means of holidays and visits. This was not the case with Aboriginal children, who, once separated, seldom found their way back to their homes and families. Obviously, that distinction underscored the differing objectives - the removal of white children was certainly a matter of protection and welfare, while the removal of Aborigine children was for the explicit purpose of social engineering. A report of the Aborigines Welfare Board produced in 1911 observed the following: "On the other hand, unless some prompt measures are taken, the children who are now growing up, will, in a few years, be in the same position as their parents. Of these children, a number who are half-castes, quadroons and octoroons, are increasing with alarming rapidity. To allow these children to remain on the reserves, to grow up in comparative idleness, and in the midst of more or less vicious surroundings would be, to say the least, an injustice to the children themselves, and a positive menace to the state."

The problem of half-castes occupied the minds of colonial authorities across the British Empire. Miscegenation was a problem particularly acute in the African colonies, and a sense existed that the governing race had an obligation to ensure that those unfortunates thus born had every opportunity to rise to the potentialities of their white blood. Thus, many of these children ended up was in schools or homes specifically established for the purpose of reconfiguring their cultural orientation.

The general policy of segregation saw the creation of Aboriginal reserves, beginning in the closing decades of the 19th century. In this regard, the policy was simply to keep Aboriginal populations separate from European populations. This was a policy that found favor in many parts of the empire, and it was regarded as the "Sacred Trust" or "Dual Mandate." To an extent, it was as much to separate indigenous people for their own protection, based on the observation that modern society was deeply corrosive to traditional lifestyles. The primitive race was groping in cultural darkness towards the light of civilization, and in all respects, it was preferable that they be allowed to do so at their own pace. In practice, however, it was all simply a matter of "out of sight, out of mind."

In the case of the African colonies, it was a question of land pressure and the conflicting needs of a growing black population and a minority settler population. In Australia, however, full-blooded Aborigine population levels were declining while that of half-castes was steadily rising. The reserves, therefore, were more than just a holding pen to contain a population under customary law; instead, they intended to compel Aborigines, especially those of mixed blood, to assimilate into white society. There were some who could not and would never be assimilated, but their children very well could.

Once institutionalized, Aborigine children were isolated from their parents as a way of making sure there was a clean break. Although visits were legally provided for, most parents were unaware of this and were in any case discouraged from trying to retain contact. A vast majority of children never saw family members ever again. Children discharged from the homes and directed towards employment were generally forbidden to return to or enter the reserves, and by then, few had an interest in doing so anyway; after all, they did not know their families, or even where their families were.

As all the statutes' language suggested, the staff in the various institutions wielded disproportionate power. There has been a tendency in various historiographies to paint the entire institution as run and governed by a breed of psychopathic racists imported specifically to torture innocent Aboriginal children, but the majority were well-meaning and vocational and believed entirely in the virtue of their work. The objective was not to produce a generation of debased and scarred pseudo-Europeans, but to equip the Aboriginal people to exploit the potentialities of modern life. As abhorrent as it appears today, the concept of separation was neither vindictive nor intentionally cruel, but conceived as the most viable policy of replacing indigenous institutions destroyed by colonization. To the British, indigenous societies would likely never have practical value in a new age irreversibly estranged from the old.

The difficulties these children experienced were even worse once they were released and placed in employment. No non-white individual was ever spared from racism, and the half-castes were not fully welcome neither in Aboriginal society or in white society. At 15, children, as wards of the state, entered an apprenticeship. Girls often went into domestic service while boys usually found their way into some sort of agricultural labor. As would have been the case in the homes, a majority would have found themselves in situations where they were treated well and humanely. Under the terms of race hierarchy, they would always be an "Abo" or a "blackfella," but that did not uniformly translate into violence or ostracization.

They were paid less, and wages were held in trust and released only at the discretion of an Aboriginal affairs official. All of this tended to perpetuate stagnation, and the temporary policy of training Aboriginals to take on the lower levels of employment until they could rise by increments tended to become permanent.

By the 1920s, the preferred policy became one of forced assimilation as efforts were made to try and reduce the number of people in the reserves, in particular those of mixed race who were beginning to form the majority. No census figures existed to differentiate between full and mixed blood Aborigines, but by the late 1920s and early 1930s, a majority of those identified as Aborigines were of mixed genetic heritage. The reserves, of course, were coveted by land-hungry white agriculturalists, and pressure to decommission the reserves was felt mainly from that quarter. There were many who felt that the reserves simply served to perpetuate social decay among those living under conditions that were superficially nomadic, but in reality static and impoverished.

In many respects, this was the worst point in the history of the Aborigines. The efforts of the various protection boards and associated agencies simply created the "lost generations" phenomenon, without appreciably solving the "Aboriginal Problem," all while creating even more problems. The state of Aboriginal society was abject, alcoholism was rampant, and social decay was a fact of life. Cultural memory was gradually losing clarity, and the old ways were dying out with nothing to replace them. Very little sympathy for the plight of the Aboriginal people was felt among the white majority, and on the whole, native society was regarded as indolent, dissolute, and without hope of redemption. The full-blooded population was diminished to a few pockets here and there, and as the reserves became a thing of the past, they were replaced by itinerant encampments on the fringes of towns and cities.

The Slow Recovery

By the 1920s, Aboriginal society had begun to organize, and a number of formative associations were established that stayed active from the 1920s-1940s. Initially, efforts were made to lobby against the Aboriginal Protection Board, arguing that it should be dissolved and replaced by an organization with an all-Aborigine membership. It would, of course, be some time before Aborigines began to enter mainstream Australian politics, but organization in the modern political context was beginning to happen, and it did not take long to gather momentum.

In 1925, the "Australian Aboriginal Progress Association" was founded by Fred Maynard, a self-educated drover and trades unionist. The AAPA was the first organization to advocate on behalf of Aboriginal rights across a broad front. What is perhaps most interesting about this is that Maynard was inspired by the black Jamaican nationalist Marcus Garvey. In 1920, Marcus Garvey's "Universal Negro Improvement Association" had a branch in Sydney, and although it was not all that active there, its message was progressive. The AAPA's platform was land freehold, an end to the removal of Aboriginal children, and the abolition of the Aborigine Protection Board.

The AAPA disappeared before the end of the 1920s, and the next significant Aborigine political organization was the Australian Aborigines League, founded in Melbourne in 1934 by William Cooper. Cooper was an Aboriginal political activist and community leader, and his group was a more substantial organization that broke the ice for a handful of active Australian Aboriginals. These included Margaret Tucker, Eric Onus, Anna and Caleb Morgan, and Shadrach James, all of whom would remain active in Aboriginal activism in the years to come.

An early platform was to lobby for Aboriginal inclusion in the Federal Parliament, and in 1938, Australia Day was commemorated by a day of mourning. In 1937, the Aborigines Progressive Association was founded in New South Wales by William Ferguson and Jack Patten. The only real activity of the organization was to co-organize the same national day of mourning.

Naturally, the question of Aboriginal voting rights featured prominently on the agendas of all of these organizations. As a series of British colonies, Australia was bound by the same basic rules of franchise that governed the empire as a whole, and those rules granted rights of suffrage to all subjects of the British Crown regardless of race, color or creed. In colonies that were governed directly from Whitehall through an imperial governor, no franchise existed at all, but in most colonies settled by British subjects, a self-governing status was typically awarded, which allowed for a locally elected legislature, cabinet and premier. In cases such as these, all imperial subjects enjoyed access to the ballot if they could meet educational and property qualifications. Inevitably, those requirements tended to preclude native populations, so the Aborigines existed entirely outside the political process.

The Australian colonies began to acquire rights of self-government towards the middle of the 19th century, and in most cases, as more white men acquired voting rights, some Aboriginal Australians did too under those same basic educational and monetary qualifications. However, since almost no Aborigines were educated, and even fewer owned property in the accepted sense of the word, they tended not to enjoy widespread access to the ballot. Moreover, the Commonwealth Franchise Act 1902, which formalized the Australian Federation, creating the Commonwealth of Australia, added severe restrictions to Aboriginal access to the vote. This was amended only in 1962, after which Aborigines were in a position to vote under the same terms as any other Australian.

These voting restrictions were complicated somewhat by the uncertain status of mixed race Australians. In general, local officials were left to decide themselves who they would allow to vote and who they would not. In most cases, anyone with the slightest appearance of Aboriginal blood would be turned away from the voting booth.

The Aboriginal population remained conspicuously apathetic towards politics during the first few decades of the 20th century, and their political activism focused mostly on generating interest among those marginalized Aboriginal communities that felt wholly disinvested in the political process. Early Aboriginal political activity was focused on wresting from state control the business of managing Aboriginal affairs. In April 1937, a Commonwealth conference was convened specifically for the purpose of discussing "Aboriginal welfare," during which the whole spectrum of issues related to that subject, and Aboriginal life in general, came under discussion. In the preamble to the conference, even the definition of "native" was covered. Under a brief chapter heading, "Destiny of the Race," the official report of the conference remarked, "That this Conference believes that the destiny of the natives of aboriginal origin, but not of the full blood, lies in their ultimate absorption by the people of the Commonwealth, and it, therefore, recommends that all efforts be directed to that end."

Thus, assimilation was adopted as the official policy, but the question of identifying who was a native remained. In New South Wales, Victoria, and South Australia, so few full-blooded Aborigines survived that the question of their management was moot. The Northern Territory still hosted a small population of Aborigines, and they were to be dealt with separately. A "native," therefore, was defined as any person "of full-blood descended from the original inhabitants of Australia." These would remain under the terms of "native administration," while all others with varying degrees of white and Aboriginal blood would not be regarded as native. Instead, they would be categorized as assimilated Australians.

Given the torturous relationship between the people of Australia, the Aborigine involvement in Britain's various armed services is an interesting one. It may be somewhat surprising that Aboriginal Australians served in any of the various constabularies and militias throughout the 19th century and early 20th century, but some did.

Typically, Aborigines were engaged as trackers and guides during the Frontier Wars, and alongside Australian servicemen involved in the Anglo-Boer War were a handful of Aborigine trackers. That said, until the second half of the 20th century, non-whites were barred from entering the armed forces, so no Aborigines were formally inducted into the various military branches.

Nevertheless, during World War I, about 500 Aborigines and a few hundred Torres Strait Islanders were able to enlist. This was due to the inability of identifying who was black and who was not, and in the end, if a recruit did not look too "native," they would be allowed to sign up.

As World War I progressed and the need for more manpower grew, fewer questions tended to be asked. Aboriginal Australians were present in almost every campaign where other Australians and New Zealanders served, and under conditions of combat, traditional perceptions of race were smoothed out. Perhaps for the first time, whites and Aboriginal Australians met on a level playing field. Aboriginal soldiers did not serve in specific units, as was the case with the Māori in the New Zealand Division, so specific awards or casualty figures do not exist, but it is believed that about a third of the Aboriginal servicemen deployed overseas were killed. One particular Aboriginal soldier, Private Douglas Grant, when captured, was studied as an anthropological curiosity by German doctors before being placed in command of a camp of black prisoners of war.

Once back in Australia, military service did nothing to level out the fundamental inequalities of daily life. Demobilized Aboriginal servicemen were granted no particular recognition. However, as World War II loomed in the 1930s, there was again a surprising number of Aboriginal men and women willing to volunteer for service on behalf of the Allies. Again, despite the fact enlistment rules precluded non-whites, many found their way into the services without much difficulty.

Aboriginal and mixed-blood men received equal terms of service and pay during the war, which was something utterly unheard of in civilian life. Promotions were granted on merit, and friendships between white and Aboriginal men frequently formed. The first Aboriginal serviceman to be commissioned was Reginald Walter Saunders. Born into a military family, Saunders' father and grandfather had served in World War I and the Anglo-Boer War respectively, and Saunders himself saw action in various World War II theatres and the Korean War, ending his service with the rank of captain.

In total, some 3,000 Aboriginal Australians and Torres Strait Islanders served in the Australian armed services in World War II. A few of these served in specifically raised indigenous units, within which they were paid less and generally afforded little if any recognition at the end of the war. The majority, however, served on equal terms, though this did not translate at the end of the war to full citizenship rights or equal recognition.

During the Korean War and the fighting in Malay, Aboriginal soldiers were again present in appreciable numbers. Aborigines were deployed in all of these conflicts both in the uniformed services and as trackers and guides. In these cases, based on the environment in which the fighting was taking place, the darker skinned and more "bush" an individual appeared, the more he was sought after. Aboriginal tracking skills were regarded as almost preternatural, and in the jungles of Burma and Malaya, they operated alongside Australian and Commonwealth units from across the empire.

The second half of the 20th century brought about a sea change of attitudes on both sides of the race divide. The end of World War II had introduced mass immigration to the colonies, and hundreds of thousands of demobilized British servicemen looked to the sunshine of the colonies, even as the British Empire was on the verge of decolonization across the world. All of the British colonies registered a boost in immigration at this time, but in those such as Australia and the African colonies with large native populations, a far more intense level of racism took root.

At the same time, Indian independence, achieved in 1947, inspired liberation movements across the empire. In Australia, it was at that moment that the Aboriginal political and self-help organizations began to gather strength, and a mood of empowerment and defiance started to manifest. The edifice began to crumble in the 1940s when the New South Wales Aboriginal Protection Board was stripped of its right to remove children. It would take some time before all the states followed suit, but it was a beginning. The practice had in any case been diminishing through most of the inter-war period as Aboriginal advocacy groups gathered increasing momentum and influence.

The 1960s was a fruitful period for the movement of international liberation. Most British colonies in what might be described as the "developing world" achieved independence during this period, and in the United States, the Civil Rights Movement was reaching a crescendo. At the same time, a confluence of many different factors began to ignite a style of civil rights movement in Australia that highlighted the general condition of Aboriginal life. There were numerous threads, but one of the recurrent themes was to remove authority for Aboriginal affairs from the purview of the individual states to the government of the Commonwealth. In other words, advocates wanted a centralized, national agency responsible for Aboriginal welfare. This was also a central theme of early advocacy groups, and it was a cause taken up incrementally by women's groups, church groups, and various civil rights organizations springing up all over the Commonwealth.

In August 1944, a Commonwealth-wide referendum was held entitled the "Australian Post-War Reconstruction and Democratic Rights Referendum." One of the 14 proposed points was the "ability to legislate for indigenous Australians." The referendum failed, but the concept took a significant step forward as a consequence.

By then, the development and urbanization of white Australia markedly contrasted with the deteriorating conditions under which native Australians were increasingly finding themselves. This was particularly true in the remote areas and in the Western Desert, where not only some style of the old nomadic lifestyles survived but where also the worst degradation was evident. By the 1950s, land alienation was complete, and most Aboriginals existed in a landless condition, estranged from employment and urban development, and under social conditions resembling some of the worst regions of the developed world. Individual states controlled the lives and movements of Aboriginal people, and, of course, many were not even the legal guardians of their own children. Aboriginal adults were not even empowered to manage their own earnings.

There was very little overlap between these two worlds, but early in 1957, the report of a Parliamentary select committee, "Report of Conditions at Laverton and Warburton Ranges, December 1956," was published. Also known as the Grayden Report, it finally laid bare the facts. This report was accompanied by a silent film sequence made by Bill Grayden, a member of the Western Australia Parliament. The film was not intended to be part of the report, but it found its way into the public arena, and it alerted the general public to what was taking place. The sequence was filmed in 16mm color, and it portrayed naked children, pot-bellied with their faces covered with sores and flies. It also showed emaciated adults. Various advocacy groups obtained copies of the film, after which it was widely shown in theaters and halls all over the country.

Reaction to the screening of the film, entitled *Manslaughter*, was mixed, but it was undoubtedly sobering. It served at the very least to galvanize a renewed grassroots movement, this time led by the "Victorian Aborigines Advancement League," which was founded in 1957. The clarion call was no longer merely the centralization of Aboriginal management, but a grant for full citizenship rights for Aborigines as citizens of the Commonwealth of Australia. For the first time, the VAAL, as it was known, was not dominated by claimants to Aboriginal status (few if any full-blooded Aborigines participated in any of these early political movements), but broad-based to include many white students and activists.

In 1958, a federation of similar organizations called the "Federal Council for Aboriginal Advancement" was formed. Its ultimate objective was full rights for Aborigines, but as a necessary prelude to this, an amendment of the constitution was sought that would grant the Federal Government the power to legislate for Aboriginal people. Petitions were run, targeting the only clause of the Federal Constitution that made any mention of Aboriginal Australians at all. "The Parliament shall, subject to the Constitution, have power to make laws for the peace, order and good government of the Commonwealth with respect to the people of any race other than the aboriginal race in any State, for whom it is deemed necessary to make special laws."

A nationwide petition was begun in 1962, mounted by the Federal Council for Aboriginal Advancement, with a goal of collecting at least a quarter of a million signatures. The phrasing of this petition was rather different than that of earlier petitions, referring to "discriminations" which gave "support to other laws and regulations which deprive Aborigines of equal wages and employment opportunities and deny them the right to own and develop their remaining tribal lands." In Queensland, as an example, under the "Aborigines Preservation and Protection Act, 1939," Aboriginals could neither marry without permission nor claim legal guardianship over their own children. In Western Australia, an Aboriginal person could make a specific application for full citizenship, but this was contingent on him or her severing ties with their extended family and the broader community, a provable discharge from the army, and an absence of a communicable disease. These, and many other "discriminations," became the targets of the petition drafters.

In May 1964, Labour opposition leader Arthur Calwell introduced a Constitutional Alteration (Aborigines) Bill, which, for the first time, opened the matter for debate in Parliament. The bill, in essence, proposed that the Constitution be amended simply to remove the words "other than the aboriginal race in any State" from Section 51. Section 127, relating to census records in regards to Aborigines also came under scrutiny. The general opinion seemed to be that although it was offensive, the clause was not discriminatory. This began a separate debate over the definition of "discrimination." In much of the British Empire, discriminatory legislation was also often described as "differentiating" legislation, and under the general rule of the imperial veto, such legislation would rarely gain Crown approval. Discriminatory legislation then led to a follow-on debate about positive-discrimination.

In 1965, a group of students from the University of Sydney styled "Student Action for Aborigines" emulated the American Civil Rights Movement Freedom Riders with a bus tour through New South Wales. Moving between the towns and cities of the state, the "Freedom Ride" sought to build public awareness and garner support. The demonstration was led by the charismatic Aboriginal activist Charles Perkins. Perkins was representative of the emerging Aboriginal elite. His parents were both born to a white and an Aboriginal parent, which meant they were identified as first-generation "half-caste." His mother, Hetty Perkins, remained loyal to her tribal roots and served as an elder of the Eastern Arrernte people.

Perkins was a student of the University of Sydney, and he would be the first Aboriginal Australian to graduate from that school. Thereafter, he would be a central figure in the movement until 1967, and he remained at the forefront of Aboriginal rights advocacy until his death in October 2000.

The Freedom Ride was just one of many facets of a growing movement, and it was widely understood that the words "other than the aboriginal race in any State" was discriminatory. Although this did not necessarily overturn the prevailing opinion among legislators, it certainly did alert federal legislators to the depth of public opinion. The matter was eventually put before the Attorney General, who, in turn, advised the Cabinet to consider a referendum. Cabinet was not persuaded, but Prime Minister Robert Menzies submitted two Constitutional Alteration Bills, the first pertaining to House membership and the second advising a repeal of Section 127 as "completely out of harmony with our national attitudes."

Section 51 was not included in this bill, based on the logic that the words "other than the aboriginal race in any State" represented positive-discrimination. This might have been a defensible point, but it did not alter the fact that Section 51 was by then so deeply unpopular that its repeal was inevitable. In January 1966, under Liberal Party Prime Minister Harold Holt, the question was returned to the Parliament in the form of a Private Members Bill. For the time being, this was a simple anti-discriminatory bill preventing the Commonwealth or any state from passing legislation "which subjects any person who has been born or naturalized within the Commonwealth of Australia to any discrimination or disability within the Commonwealth by reason of his racial origin."

Again, the bill was narrowly defeated, but by then, the advocacy movement was national, highly organized, and extremely active. The movement had narrowed down to the multi-racial "Federal Council for the Advancement of Aborigines and Torres Strait Islanders," which kept the matter very much alive.

In February 1966, the "Constitution Alteration (Repeal of Section 127) Bill" was passed, which chipped away at the lower tier of the issue, leaving Section 51 standing rather lonely in the Constitution. By then it began to seem that the movement in Parliament attempting to protect the offending clause was partisan, driven by a simple unwillingness on the part of the members to climb down.

The debate now centered on the Commonwealth being granted power to "make laws for the advancement of the Aboriginal people." This prompted a bout of internal discussion on those for and against "positive discrimination," while evading the alternative solution which was simply to remove any language of race or ethnicity from the wording of the Constitution. Realizing that something needed to be done about Section 51, a referendum was again proposed. There were two main strands to the argument now. The first was that differentiating legislation amounted to discrimination, and any wording to that effect needed to be removed from the Constitution. The second was to transfer power to legislate on behalf of Aborigines to the Commonwealth while retaining the essential "differentiating" character of that power.

Either way, the writing was on the wall for Section 51. Again, the Attorney General put forward a recommendation that a referendum be held, and this time Cabinet agreed. The Federal Council for the Advancement of Aborigines and Torres Strait Islanders went straight to work, backed up by a strong majority of churches and civic organizations. The press feasted on a lively public debate, and in the age of "Letters to the Editor," public opinion appeared to be evenly divided. For the first time, the electronic and printed media opened up spaces for Aboriginal spokespeople, and Aboriginal viewers were presented in an organized, coherent, and powerful manner. This came as a surprise to many whites who knew Aborigines only as semi-literate farmhands or degenerate camp dwellers.

The referendum was held on May 27, 1967, by which time both sides had spoken. The question was posed as follows: "DO YOU APPROVE the proposed law for the alteration of the Constitution entitled— 'An Act to alter the Constitution so as to omit certain words relating to the People of the Aboriginal Race in any State and so that Aboriginals are to be counted in reckoning the population?'"

When the votes were counted, "Yes" emerged victorious. Alterations to Section 51 and 127 of the Constitution garnered about 90% of the vote, with majorities in every state. This was certainly a profound moment in the history of Aboriginal Australians, and the size of the majority was no less profound. Charles Perkins, then Vice-President of the Federal Council for the Advancement of Aborigines and Torres Strait Islanders, described it as "the moment of truth whether the white people really are interested in our welfare or rights."

The two main outcomes of the referendum were to give the Federal Government scope to act, and to give Aboriginal people a powerful moral impetus to act on their own behalf, with evidence for the first time of a political victory achieved thanks largely to their own efforts. This opened an entire spectrum of organizations, associations and movements, with agendas ranging from a review of established land policies to a revision of Aboriginal land rights.

Charles Perkins, and many others from both sides, then shifted their attention to the various committees and discussion groups that formed to guide the Federal government in the direction of implanting policies to benefit Aboriginal people. From there, things moved quickly. In 1968, the Federal "Office of Aboriginal Affairs" was established, and a year later, the New South Wales Aboriginal Welfare Board was abolished. In 1971, the first Aboriginal senator, Neville Bonner, was sworn in, and a year later, five years after the referendum, the "Aboriginal Tent Embassy" was erected on the lawns of the Federal Building in Canberra. This was a symbolic protest against the slow pace of land rights and discrimination issues. A Royal Commission was authorized to look into the land rights issue, but it was redundant almost at the moment that it was convened. This was the commencement of a far more muscular phase of Aboriginal activism, and issues of land, welfare, discrimination and rights would move to their next phase under Aboriginal impetus.

In 1994, a group of nine members of the Pintupi people made contact with the outside world for the first time. Living an entirely traditional, nomadic lifestyle in Australia's Gibson Desert, they had no previous experience of modern life and had never seen a white man. The Pintupi Nine were the last verified group of fully indigenous Aboriginals living lives unchanged from their ancestors. Their contact with the outside world marked the end of their traditional life, and for better or worse, they became assimilated Australians.

The Māori in Politics

"It is in itself a Māori custom – revenge – plunder to avenge a wrong. It was their chiefs who ceded that right to the Queen. The confiscations cannot therefore be objected to in the light of the Treaty." - Sir Āpirana Ngata

As a basic principle, all British subjects, regardless of creed, race, or religion, enjoyed equal rights in the colonies, which meant in practice that every British subject enjoyed access to the franchise. This had always been a basic tenet of British imperial overseas rule, but it was often flaunted and undermined within the colonies themselves.

New Zealand was unusually liberal in this regard. In fact, the Māori enjoyed universal suffrage sometime before white men, and women in New Zealand were the first to enjoy the vote anywhere in the world, 27 years before women in the United States.

The anomaly of Māori access to voting had to do with the superimposition of Māori constituencies over the existing electoral structure, which offered the Māori a degree of representation in early parliaments unheard of anywhere in the British Empire. In the Cape Colony of South Africa, a color-blind franchise existed from the earliest British engagement in the region, but this never resulted in a black member of parliament, and most blacks were in any case disqualified by education and property rights that a majority of them could not meet.

Despite their rights, the Māori were initially apathetic, and a majority of them did not immediately avail themselves of access to the franchise, so the system was imperfect. However, as the century progressed, more Māori began to engage with the electoral system, and in 1893, the Electoral Act opened the franchise to white women and Māori women. That said, the electoral systems remained entirely separate, with only mixed-blood citizens having the opportunity to decide which electoral system they wished to be absorbed into. It would not be until 1967 that Māori were permitted to stand for election in traditionally white constituencies. The seven reserve Māori seats and the separate Māori electorate remain a unique and controversial feature of the New Zealand electoral system.

As Māori members began to appear in the legislature, a system of party politics had yet to be established. In 1891, however, the Liberal Party was formed as the first organized political party in the colony. It governed from 1891 until 1912, and most of the Māori MPs belonged to it. During that time, a second party, the Reform Party, was founded, and in 1916, the Labour Party was founded. The Liberal party remained the favored Māori party, even though its ideology was something of a continuum of past policy insofar as it advocated the acquisition of Māori land for the resettlement of white landowners, whether by acquiring their land outright or granting it to white settlers on generous terms of credit to lay the foundation of a liberal, white landowning class. While the emphasis was on the continued acquisition of Māori land, the general ideological basis of the Liberal Party certainly was liberal in the sense that it welcomed Māori participation, and initially, it found favor among Māori voters and prospective MPs.

Perhaps the most prominent and influential Māori Member of Parliament and Liberal Party member was lawyer Sir Āpirana Ngata. Sir Āpirana Ngata was also one of the first Māori university graduates, graduating from Canterbury University in 1897 with a degree in law, after which he was admitted to the New Zealand Bar. His main political objective was the protection and preservation of Māori culture, which was already beginning to merge and assimilate into the general population to the alarm of the conservative Māori establishment.

Another was Māui Pōmare, a member of the Reform Party, also a somewhat liberal group, and his political achievements were largely related to Māori health and education. However, he also negotiated land removals, which added a touch of controversy to his career.

Sir James Carroll, known to the Māori as Timi Kara, was of mixed Māori-Irish descent. He was elected to Parliament in 1887 and served briefly as acting Colonial Secretary, the imperial equivalent to the portfolio of interior minister. He was the first Māori to serve in the New Zealand cabinet.

Sir Āpirana Ngata

In 1900, the Māori Councils Act established Māori councils and committees in almost every Māori district in New Zealand, which gave the Māori far greater control of local affairs. In the early 1930s, Sir Āpirana Ngata was largely responsible for overhauling the Native Department under a broader economic development strategy. The objective was to complete the transfer of Māori from traditional lifestyles and poor urban settlements into a phase of development that would hopefully improve housing and urbanization. Sir Āpirana Ngata and others were not always enlightened when it came to their political attitudes and policies, but they recognized that a return to the utopian past was an impractical aspiration and that the future lay in adapting and assimilating into the modern system.

The Māori in War

"I have always found them of a brave, noble, open and benevolent disposition, but they are a people that will never put up with an insult if they have an opportunity to resent it." – Captain James Cook

In many British and other European coloniesthe involvement of natives in one form or another in World War I was taken for granted.[10] While the governments of both Australia and New Zealand were concerned more with their own regional security preoccupations than defending the British Empire, the response of their expatriate populations was immediate and positive. It is also true that most colonies had some sort of a native regiment or constabulary to augment white manpower in frontier security and law and order, and as regular formations, they fought where they were ordered to fight.

No such thing was true in New Zealand, where greater indigenous political independence offered the Māori the opportunity to enlist or not, in common with every other citizen. It does, however, almost go without saying that a strong interest in the war was expressed by some who in past years would have formed the warrior class. Regardless of the political overtones, war was war, and an opportunity to fight was not to be missed. Others took a more political position and stood opposed to the war as a "white man's war" in which they had no stake.

It is interesting to note that all four Māori MPs at the time supported Māori participation in the war, and the MP for the Northern Māori, Te Rangi Hīroa, was one of the first to enlist, sailing with the first contingent of New Zealand troops in February 1915. When later asked about this, Te Rangi Hīroa remarked that he hoped that acts of Māori patriotism would foster a sense of identity with New Zealand as it was, and not longing for a past long gone. If tribalism could be broken down in favor of nationalism, all would benefit.

A majority of the Māori who fought in the war served with the "Native Contingent" of the New Zealand Expeditionary Force. The first contingent of about 500 men left Wellington in February 1915, with Te Rangi Hīroa among them. A Native Contingent Committee was established, including the MPs Āpirana Ngata and Maui Pōmare, with the responsibility of raising and

---

[10] The name "Martial Race" derives from a British classification during the North West Frontier Wars of India, during which the many cultures and ethnicities were designated either as Martial or non-Martial, according to their proclivities for war. The Gurkha, for example, were a "Martial Race," as were the Zulu, and, of course, the Māori.

reinforcing the contingent. There was a determination on the part of these men, and others of the Committee, that the Māori recruited for service see action. At the time, however, there was a concern among certain sectors of the white community that arming Māori and sending them into battle against other white European troops would somehow undermine the balance of ethnic accommodation in New Zealand. Quite a number of other colonies expressed the same concern, with leaders believing that if natives were given the opportunity to fight and kill white men in battle, the aura of European superiority would somehow be compromised.

Be that as it may, mounting casualties and difficulties in keeping the New Zealand Expeditionary Force up to strength ensured that many Māori soldiers were eventually pulled off garrison duty and sent to the front. The Gallipoli Campaign was where the New Zealand Expeditionary Force was most actively engaged, and the Māori Contingent arrived at Anzac Cove on July 3, 1915 and was merged as a separate unit of the Expeditionary force. Historians and sociologists have debated ever since what effect this battlefield interaction had on white-Māori relations, with some arguing that the experience broke down barriers and served to introduce Māori and British men to one another for the first time. Others tend to scoff at this, pointing out that Māori men embraced the sport of rugby with both aptitude and enthusiasm, and that the two groups met regularly on rugby fields all over New Zealand for decades.

Conscription, when it came, was initially restricted to whites, but this created something of a controversy. Māori leaders reminded their white counterparts that Māori blood had been shed overseas, and utu was demanded. Thus, in June 1917, conscription was extended to Māori men, but it was selectively applied to certain groups who had so far resisted voluntary calls to arms. The idea was to balance the contributions, but in the end, it simply created deeper divisions, and a great many resisters held out through both World War I and World War II.

In addition to those who fought at the front, another specific Māori contingent was the New Zealand Pioneer Battalion, which was a mixed battalion deployed mainly in battlefield engineering, labor, trench digging, and other similar tasks. It was the first New Zealand contingent to arrive on the Western Front, where much of its work was in trench digging. The Pioneer Battalion fought in the Somme and Messines.

World War II witnessed a more dedicated Māori engagement, with the establishment in 1940 of the 28th (Māori) Battalion of the New Zealand Army. Senior members of the Māori leadership urged full and unconditional Māori involvement in the war, while the resisters from before also tended to resist fighting in World War II. Again, it was Sir Āpirana Ngata who stood at the fore of the patriotic movement, arguing again that participation in war was a necessary condition of imperial citizenship. He said, "We are participants in a great Commonwealth, to the defense of which we cannot hesitate to contribute our blood and our lives. We are the possessors of rights which we must qualify to exercise, also of obligations which the Māori must discharge always in the future as he has done in the past…We are of one house, and if our Pākehā brothers fall, we fall with them. How can we ever hold up our heads, when the struggle is over, to the question, 'Where were you when New Zealand was at war?'" In essence, if the Māori wanted a greater voice in national affairs, then equal participation in the war was essential.

Sir Āpirana Ngata urged the colonial government and the defense establishment to raise a specific Māori battalion for service overseas. The government agreed, and the 28th Battalion was formed. The Battalion was organized along tribal lines, with four companies comprising recruits from all of the major tribal groupings. Enlistment was voluntary, and it remained so even after conscription was introduced at the end of May 1940.

Of course, the 28th Battalion was not the only formation within which Māori served; among the 16,000 or so Māori who registered for duty, most served in areas such as home defense, engineering, and service corps, but the few thousand who served with the 28th carried the flag for the Māori and for New Zealand in all of the major campaigns.

The Battalion saw action in Greece, Crete, North Africa and Italy, and it was distinguished for receiving more individual bravery decorations than any other New Zealand contingent. Perhaps the most noteworthy award went to Second Lieutenant Moana-Nui-a-Kiwa Ngarimu, who was recommended for the coveted Victoria Cross thanks to his actions in Tunisia on March 26, 1943, during the closing stages of the North Africa Campaign. The award would be given to him posthumously because he was killed the following day. Ngarimu was the first Māori to win the Victoria Cross, and several other candidates were put forward.

Another interesting event featured the involvement of Royal New Zealand Air Force Officer Porokoru Patapu (Johnny) Pohe in the Great Escape, a famous escape from the German prisoner of war camp Stalag Luft III. Pohe was one of the tunnelers, and one of the 76 men who escaped on the night of March 24-25, 1944. This iconic episode of the war was immortalized in a 1963 blockbuster movie. Johnny Pohe would go on to fly bombers over Germany before being shot down in September 1943. He was recaptured a few days later, along with most of the escapees, and executed by the Gestapo.

Throughout the war, the 28th Battalion maintained a strength of about 3,600 men. By the time the unit disbanded in January 1946, 649 were killed and 1,712 had been wounded.

Conclusion

In the years after the Musket Wars and the New Zealand Wars, there was a feeling within Māori society, and within New Zealand society at large, that the Māori were doomed as a unique race and would gradually lose ground to assimilation until they merged with white society. Indeed, a degree of cultural apathy certainly did follow the Māori into the 20th century. In 1840, the estimates of the Māori population ran to a figure of between 40,000 and 70,000, against a white population of about 2,000. By the turn of the century, however, whites numbered about

700,000 and Māori no more than 50,000, having crept back up a bit from a low in 1860 of 37,500.

Population levels gradually stabilized and began to edge to a figure of about 82,000 in the early 1930s, but the lines of distinct Māori lineage began to merge as substantial levels of intermarriage took place. To date, there are very few pure Māori remaining in New Zealand, to the extent that it was newsworthy in 2017 when media presenter Oriini Kaipara was identified by DNA as "full-blood Māori."

Even as assimilation and intermarriage have taken place, the Māori identity in New Zealand is very strong, and a cultural revival has taken place in recent years through a reevaluation of the Treaty of Waitangi and other colonial-era treaties. This has fostered a widespread protest movement and a resurgence in interest in native property rights and various avenues of restitution. The 2013 New Zealand census recorded 598,605 people who identified as Māori, while 668,724 claimed Māori descent. This amounts to about 15% and 17% percent of the overall population of New Zealand, respectively. Pockets of expatriate Māori populations also reside in Australia, the United Kingdom, Canada and the United States.

One of the most divisive New Zealand political issues remains the reserved Māori seats in Parliament, with renewed calls for the abolition of the practice every time a general election is held. Nonetheless, the practice continues to this day.

Online Resources

Other titles about Aborigines on Amazon

Other titles about New Zealand on Amazon

Further Reading

Bach, John (1976). A Maritime History of Australia. Melbourne: Nelson. ISBN 0-17005087-4.

Barker, Anthony. What Happened When: A Chronology of Australia from 1788. Allen & Unwin. 2000. online edition

Bambrick, Susan ed. The Cambridge Encyclopedia of Australia (1994)

Basset, Jan The Oxford Illustrated Dictionary of Australian History (1998)

Broeze, Frank (1998). Island Nation: A History of Australians and the Sea. Sydney: Allen & Unwin. ISBN 9781864484243.

Davison, Graeme, John Hirst, and Stuart Macintyre, eds. The Oxford Companion to Australian History (2001) online at many academic libraries; also excerpt and text search

Galligan, Brian, and Winsome Roberts, eds. Oxford Companion to Australian Politics (2007); online at many academic libraries

Lewis, Wendy, Simon Balderstone and John Bowan (2006). Events That Shaped Australia. New Holland. ISBN 978-1-74110-492-9.

O'Shane, Pat et al. Australia: The Complete Encyclopedia (2001)

Serle. Percival, ed. Dictionary of Australian Biography (1949)online edition

Shaw, John, ed. Collins Australian Encyclopedia (1984)

Taylor, Peter. The Atlas of Australian History (1991)

Connor, John (2002). The Australian frontier wars, 1788–1838. Sydney: UNSW Press. ISBN 0-86840-756-9

James Belich, Making Peoples: A History of the New Zealanders from the Polynesian settlement to the end of the 19th century (1996)

James Belich, Paradise Reforged: A History of the New Zealanders from 1880 to the Year 2000 (2001).

Giselle Byrnes, ed. (2009). The New Oxford History of New Zealand. Oxford University Press.

Michael King (2003) The Penguin History of New Zealand.

Leveridge, Steven. "Another Great War? New Zealand interpretations of the First World War towards and into the Second World War" First World War Studies (2016) 7#3:303-25.

Parsons, Gwen. "The New Zealand Home Front during World War One and World War Two." History Compass 11.6 (2013): 419-428.

Smith, Philippa Mein. A Concise History of New Zealand (Cambridge Concise Histories) (2nd ed. 2012)

Keith Sinclair, ed., (1996) The Oxford Illustrated History of New Zealand.

Keith Sinclair, A History of New Zealand.

Ranginui Walker (2004), Ka Whawhai Tonu Matou: Struggle Without End.

Free Books by Charles River Editors

We have brand new titles available for free most days of the week. To see which of our titles are currently free, click on this link.

Discounted Books by Charles River Editors

We have titles at a discount price of just 99 cents everyday. To see which of our titles are currently 99 cents, click on this link.

Made in the USA
Columbia, SC
13 March 2020